MARGARET BOYLES'

Designs for Babies

A FIRESIDE BOOK   Published by Simon & Schuster, Inc.   New York

First Fireside Edition, 1984

Published by Simon & Schuster, Inc.
Simon & Schuster Building
Rockefeller Center
1230 Avenue of the Americas
New York, New York 10020

FIRESIDE and colophon are registered trademarks of Simon & Schuster, Inc.

Designed by Edith Fowler

Manufactured in the United States of America

10 9 8 7 6 5 4 3 2 1
10 9 8 7 6 5 4 3 2 1 Pbk.

Library of Congress Cataloging in Publication Data

Boyles, Margaret
  Margaret Boyles' designs for babies.

  1. Needlework—Patterns. 2. Infants—Clothing.
I. Title. II. Title: Designs for babies.
TT753.B68   1983   746.4   82-25596

ISBN 0-671-43902-2
ISBN 0-671-53028-3 Pbk.

Contents

This book is for my first granddaughter, Meagan Michelle Eastman, my "Beauty" who has inherited, worn and given her approval to the designs in the book. She is a miracle and a delight in herself, thus adding much to my own pleasure in presenting this collection of baby finery for you to make for your own baby.

Introduction

This is a happy book written for the happiest of people—mothers, grandmothers, aunts, and friends waiting for the birth of a new baby. It is a book full of the anticipation only they can feel, and it responds to their longings to begin making tiny garments immediately and to poke through old trunks of clothing that belonged to generations past, either to salvage or to copy beloved little things worn by babies of bygone days, thus linking the generations in a chain of love.

When work on this book began, no excitement of a new grandchild coming inspired the clicking of knitting needles, but this was a project I had long wanted to carry out. Embroidery and the construction of baby clothing has long been dear to my heart, and a trunk full to overflowing with lovely things worn by my four children often reminded me that these ideas and designs should be

shared. The recent trend to mixing nostalgic old sewing techniques and patterns with modern fabrics and practical designs made the time seem right for a book like this.

It was the end of winter—Atlanta's special gray, cold two months that magically break into the most breathtaking spring imaginable—when I started making a list of projects to be included in the book. I unpacked the old trunk holding my treasure of baby clothing and spread the tiny garments on the pink studio carpet. It was a happy, nostalgic time and I admit not much work was done that day.

Every piece I unpacked held special memories. A yellow silk sacque and bonnet conjured up the memory of the precious baby boy who wore them home from the hospital on a cold April day in Boston—home to an apartment on campus at MIT, where his father would be graduated in another month. Then I took out a handmade dress of palest green—the favorite color of a grandfather who had shopped long until he found green in those days when baby clothes were either white, pink, or blue. His delight in seeing Baby Nancy wear it is as dear a memory to me as her dancing black eyes and brown curls. A pink knit sacque, bonnet, and mittens were next, bought in Mexico by that same grandfather for another little girl, saved not only because they were so pretty and held so many memories, but also because the lovely raglan yoke of the sacque was knitted in a raised leaf design that should someday be copied.

I also found a long dress and slip made for my mother when she was a baby. My grandmother could never decide why that particular dress had survived when all the "good" ones had disappeared. This one was made by machine—a terrible transgression, she thought—but it is lovely with its rows and rows of tucks, tiny eyelet yoke, and wide, embroidered ruffle.

Mixed in with all the others were several batiste dresses, slips, a yellowed wool sacque, and a pair of black buttoned shoes that I had worn as an infant. There were also many homely, utilitarian articles I have never known why I saved; now that they are this old, I'll continue to keep them regardless of their value.

Some of the most precious things of all were the soft batiste day gowns and dresses my grandmother made for my first baby. I can still see her getting the bolt of batiste from the shelf in the linen closet, cutting her own paper pattern, and sitting contentedly in her old red-leather rocking chair while she hand-stitched and tucked for hours at a time. Every seam is a French seam, pin tucks and whipped tucks abound, rows of delicate Feather Stitching trim collars and hems, hemstitching adorns tiny yokes, and lace and insertions are attached with stitches so fine you can hardly find them.

I sometimes wonder if as she sewed my grandmother knew her stitches would survive her. Did she think about having made the same little garments for her own children, grandchildren, and again for her great-grandchildren? Did she wonder if still another generation might wear the precious little gowns she was stitching with such love?

The treasures in the trunk are many, all holding memories, all dear. Some have inspired pieces in this book, but none has actually been exactly reproduced. Kent's yellow sacque is pure silk and lovely, but so impractical; the pink quilted one it inspired in this book looks just as delicate but, thanks to easy-care fabric, it can be used and enjoyed without worry. The little boy's suits are very similar to the classic button-ons worn by generations of little boys but are made with new blended easy-care fabrics where possible. The two comforters are made of the same practical fabrics, one in a contemporary graphic design, the other in an adaptation of an old idea. The bibs are cut from a quilted material that would have amazed our grandmothers but is so easy to buy we hardly think about it. The bassinet, a ruffled and tucked bit of whimsy, would have been a major project to keep looking fresh without the wonders of polyester, but even with its modern fabric it has a look that could have come right out of a turn-of-the-century magazine.

About half of the work for the book had been completed when my husband and I received the exciting news that we would be grandparents in the spring—just about the time the manuscript was due to be finished. That added to the pleasure of making and describing articles for the book and also resulted in the addition of some very practical things like flannel sheets, receiving blankets, and bibs. Happily, a baby will use most of the things pictured. As I finish typing this note to my readers, the book is scheduled to be shipped on the baby's birthday. A most fitting ending for a happy year!

I'm certain that by the time you've gotten around to reading this you've looked at the pictures of the projects and maybe even made several of them. You've noticed that I've included knitting, Heirloom Sewing, counted cross stitch, crewel embroidery, machine sewing, stuffed toys, quilting, appliqué and delicate embroidery to put together a collection of memorable baby layette necessities, toys and tiny frills. While this is not intended as a beginner's instruction book teaching the basics of all the skills used, you will find that the instructions are detailed and clear enough to allow easy duplication of the pictured models. Just for extra measure, the Techniques Appendix contains ad-ditional information about Heirloom Sewing and some of the most important methods used for this lovely old art. There are details included to make construction of the clothing easier and I hope that if you have not tried this sewing recently, you read that chapter before beginning to cut or sew. I've also added a few notes about knitting and a list of the abbreviations I use. If you have basic skills and understand the language of knitting, sewing and embroidery, you are on your way to making your baby some very special clothing and toys.

I could have easily spent another year on the book making all manner of pretty baby clothes—a christening dress and slip, smocked day gowns, more sweaters, a bunting for a winter baby, more stuffed toys, other designs in wall hangings and comforters, the list could go on and on. But time catches up with us and space in a book is necessarily limited, so I have chosen this collection as an inspiration and suggestion of the lovely baby things that can be made with a little time and effort. My heartfelt wish is that you will enjoy making the designs and find much happiness in using or giving them. If you are waiting for a new baby, I hope this book adds to your pleasures of anticipation—may your baby be as perfect and as special as I know ours is going to be. Happy waiting and happy stitching!

Margaret Boyles

PROJECTS

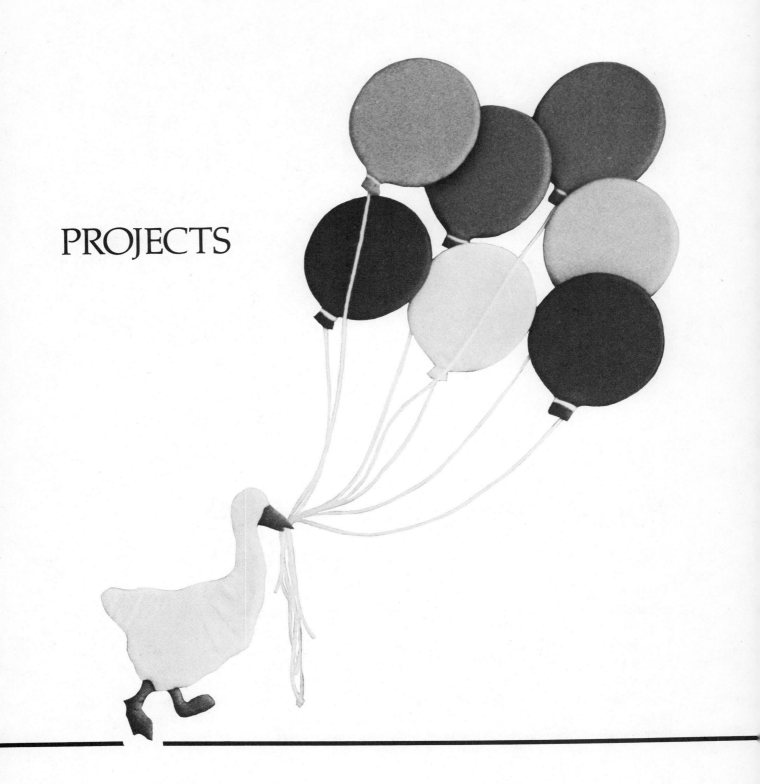

Heirloom Pillow

To begin any new sewing or embroidery technique, it is usually a good idea to practice by making a sampler, to learn the working methods, experiment with them, and find if the technique is something in which you really want to invest time and money before plunging into a large and expensive project. This dainty baby pillow, which utilizes most of the Heirloom Sewing tech-

niques, can function as an Heirloom sampler but when finished it will be a useful and lovely baby gift or accessory worthy of the time and effort expended on it.

Babies don't sleep on pillows, of course, but this one will quickly find its place in the nursery or carriage and will be cherished and more than likely used on a little girl's bed for many years.

SIZE
9½ × 12 inches (excluding ruffle)

MATERIALS
Batiste, white, 45 inches wide, ⅝ yard
Lace edging, ½ inch wide, 3 yards
Lace beading, ½ inch wide, 1⅛ yards
Entredeux, white, 3⅝ yards
Ribbon, pale blue, ¼ inch wide, 1¼ yards
Embroidery floss, pale blue, ¼ skein
Buttons, ¼ inch diameter, white pearl, 2

INSTRUCTIONS
If this is your first experiment with Heirloom Sewing, please read the comments about it in the Techniques on page 122 before beginning to cut or sew. In that section you will find directions for all the stitches needed, information about rolling, whipping and attaching lace as well as instructions for making puffing strips, seams, etc. With the information in that section, plus your own basic knowledge of sewing, you can make this lovely decorative pillow for your baby.

Look for the best quality white batiste you can find. Several kinds imported from Switzerland have a fine thread count and a slightly glazed look; these are excellent for this type of sewing.

Cut all pieces for the pillow on lines marked by pulling threads. Cut the following pieces, laying them out on the fabric as suggested on the cutting diagram: three panels, 4½ × 11 inches; two backs, 8 × 11 inches; two puffing strips, 2½ × 22 inches; and 100 inches of ruffles, 3 inches wide, in pieces as suggested on the diagram.

The three panels measuring 4½ × 11 inches are for the center and two side pieces of the pillow front. Roll and whip the 11-inch sides of one for the center panel, then whip entredeux to the rolled edges.

Fold a piece of tracing paper in half. Open it flat and match the fold line to the slashed line on the drawing for the center-panel embroidery motif. Trace the motif and curved lines as shown, omitting the four little dots at the sides of the curved lines—these are guides for placement of the little flowers on the side panels.

Fold the paper again on the fold line and trace the pattern through the paper to make a complete design. Go over the outlines with a transfer pencil; with a hot iron, stamp the design on the fabric, centering it on the panel. Embroider using the stitches noted and a single strand of embroidery floss. When you are finished, if any traces of the transfer pattern show, wash the panel carefully in cool water and iron dry.

Whip lace beading to the entredeux on each side of the embroidered center panel.

Roll, whip, and gather both sides of the puffing strips. Pull up the fullness so each strip

puffing		puffing			
back	back	cent. panel	side panel	side panel	ruffle
					ruffle
ruffle					
ruffle					

CUTTING DIAGRAM FOR HEIRLOOM PILLOW

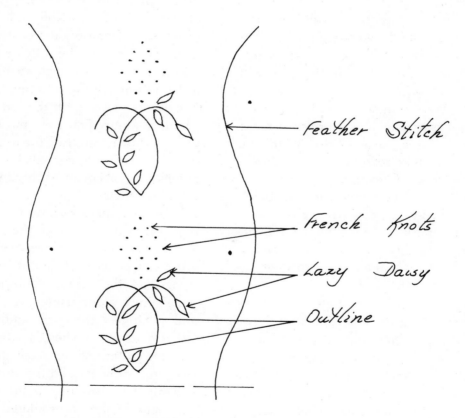

Feather Stitch

French Knots

Lazy Daisy

Outline

EMBROIDERY MOTIF FOR HEIRLOOM PILLOW

measures 11 inches. Whip entredeux to both sides of each strip. Join the entredeux to the lace beading on both sides of center panel.

Whip a second row of lace beading to the entredeux on the unattached edge of the puffing strips.

Roll, whip, and attach entredeux to one long side of each side panel. Fold each panel in half vertically and mark the center point at either end. Measure out ½ inch on each side of the center point, then mark and pull threads for two tucks placed ½ inch apart. (The first tuck will be ½ inch from the center mark, the second ½ inch from the first.) Stitch the four tucks and press them toward the outside edges.

Lightly trace the wavy line at the side of the center-panel drawing down the middle of the space between the tucks. Mark the dots on the curves of the lines as a guide for placing the flowers. With a single strand of blue embroidery floss, work a row of very small Feather Stitches on the wavy line. At each dot make a flower composed of five small Lazy Daisy Stitches surrounding a single French Knot.

Press the panels—if necessary, wash the panels first to remove any traces of embroidery markings and then wet-press. Attach the entredeux along the side edges of the panels to the lace beading on the sides of the puffing strips.

Insert ribbon in the four rows of lace beading. Tack ends to hold ribbon in place.

Roll and whip a hem on one 11-inch side of each of the back pieces. Turn this rolled edge back to form a 1-inch hem on each piece. Place one piece over the other so that just the hems overlap. Baste through the hems. Using a French seam, join pillow front to back.

French-seam the ruffle pieces to form a strip 100 inches long. Join the ends with another French seam to make a circle. Roll and whip one edge, attaching the lace edging to it without gathering the lace.

Cut a strip of entredeux to fit around the outside edge of the pillow. Roll and gather the other edge of the ruffle to fit the entredeux. Whip the entredeux to the gathered edge of the ruffle. Whip the entredeux to the outside of the pillow.

Make two buttonholes in the back opening of the pillow. Sew on buttons.

Make a 9½ × 12-inch pillow form from white muslin. Stuff it with fiberfill and insert it into pillow case.

HEIRLOOM PILLOW DETAIL. Reading from the left, this detail of the Heirloom Pillow (project on page 14) shows puffing, ribbon-threaded lace beading with entredeux attached to both edges; the embroidered center panel; another row of lace beading and entredeux; a puffing strip; a repeat of the lace beading; and the tucked and embroidered side panel.

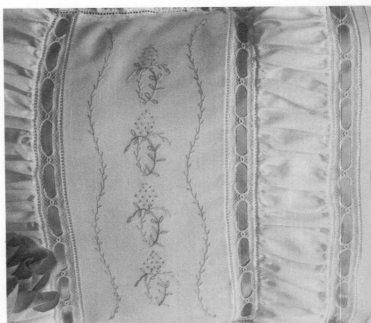

Heirloom Dress and Slip

Every baby girl is born a princess in the eyes of her family—and she seems to know that from the very beginning, too! Here for your most royal little princess is a dress worthy of her station.

Although the pattern itself is one of the most basic, it is embellished with lace, insertion, ribbon, and ruffles to delight the most feminine of tastes. This is a party dress, a dress-up dress, a go-to-visit-Grandma dress, a dress even a tiny girl will enjoy.

DRESS

SIZE
Six months

MATERIALS
Batiste, white, 45 inches wide, 1⅜ yards
Lace insertion, ¼ inch wide, 9 yards
Lace edging, ½ inch wide, 9 yards
Entredeux, white, 4 yards
Lace beading, ½ inch wide, 2½ yards
Embroidery floss, white, ¼ skein
Sewing thread, white cotton
Buttons, baby-size, white, 3
Ribbon, white, ¼ inch wide, 2 yards

INSTRUCTIONS

If this is your first experiment with Heirloom Sewing, please read the comments about it on page 122 in the Techniques before beginning to cut or sew. In that section you will find directions for all the stitches needed, information about rolling, whipping and attaching lace, as well as instructions for other sewing techniques necessary for completing this sweet dress for your own baby girl.

All seam allowances are ¼ inch, as noted on the pattern pieces. Cut on the solid lines. Unless otherwise noted, all seams should be French seams.

Note that the pattern pieces for yokes and sleeves show a rectangle of fabric with the outline of the pattern within. It is much preferable to work on the rectangle, inserting the trim before cutting out the pattern shapes.

Using pulled threads to mark cutting lines, cut the following pieces:

1 yoke front, 9½ × 4¼ inches
2 yoke backs, 6 × 4¼ inches
2 sleeves, 15 × 5 inches
2 skirt pieces, 27 × 7½ inches
3 ruffle strips, 3 × 45 inches

YOKE FRONT

Measure up 1 inch from a long side of the yoke rectangle, pull a thread, and cut on the resulting line. Roll, whip, and attach lace insertion to one edge of the larger piece. Whip beading to the insertion, then another row of insertion to the beading. Roll one edge of the other yoke section and whip it to the free edge of the lace insertion.

With a single strand of white embroidery floss, work a row of tiny Feather Stitches close to the rolled edges above and below the insertion. Press well. Place the pattern piece on the yoke rectangle, centering it and keeping the bottom edges even. With a washable fabric marker, trace the outlines of the pattern. Reinforce the stitching at the armholes where it crosses the cutting line. Cut out the yoke.

Roll the bottom edge of the yoke and attach entredeux to it.

With care not to stretch the fabric, roll both shoulder seam allowances and attach entredeux. (If you prefer, these shoulder seams can be French seams, but the entredeux treatment is very dainty and special.)

Insert ribbon in the beading and tack the ends in place.

YOKE BACKS

Repeat the procedures for the yoke front on the two back pieces. Turn facings to the inside on the fold lines and press. Finish the facing edges with a rolled hem. Roll the bottom edges and attach entredeux. Roll the shoulder seams and attach to the entredeux on the yoke-front seams.

SLEEVES

Measure up ¾ inch from the bottom edge of the sleeve rectangle and pull a thread. Pull two more threads, each ¾ inch above the last.

Cut the sleeve rectangles apart on the middle line. Roll both edges and whip in one row of lace insertion. Make ⅛ inch pin tuck on each of the other lines. Feather Stitch along the rolled edges above and below the

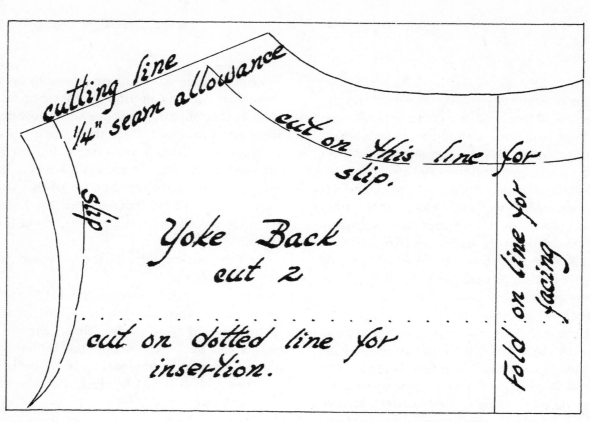

cutting line

1/4" seam allowance

cut on this line for slip.

slip

Fold on line for facing

Yoke Back
cut 2

cut on dotted line for insertion.

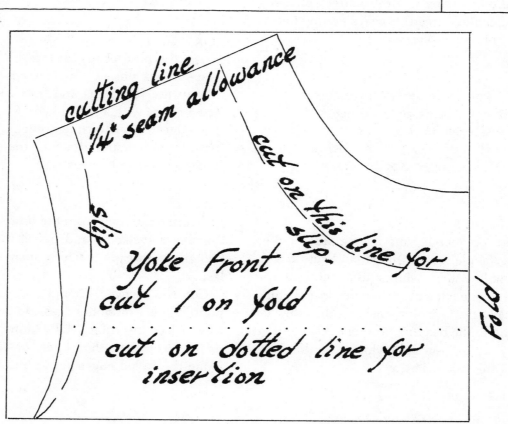

cutting line

1/4" seam allowance

cut on this line for slip.

slip

Fold

Yoke Front
cut 1 on fold

cut on dotted line for insertion

PATTERN FOR HEIRLOOM DRESS

insertion to match yokes. Press tucks away from the insertion.

Following the instruction for cutting the yoke front, cut out the sleeves. Roll, whip, and gather the lower edge to 7½ inches. Attach a strip of entredeux. Whip a row of lace insertion to the entredeux. Gather the lace edging and whip to the insertion to make a full ruffle.

SKIRT

With wrong sides together, lay the front and back skirt pieces on a flat surface. Trace the armhole cutting guide on a piece of paper. Lay the cutting guide at the top left corner of the skirt pieces, matching the top and side seams to those marked on the guide. Cutting through both layers of fabric, cut out the curved bottom of the armhole. Repeat in reverse at the top right corner of the skirt pieces.

Fold one skirt piece in half and mark the top center. Cut a 3 inch opening on the fold line for a back placket. Cut a 1 × 6½-inch bias strip and finish the placket opening with a continuous lap.

From the bottom edge of each skirt piece measure up 3¼ inches, pull a thread, and cut apart on the line. Roll, whip, and attach lace insertion to the top sections. Whip a row of lace beading to the insertion. Feather Stitch along the rolled edge.

Measure up ¾ inch from the rolled edge and pull a thread. Pull two more threads above the first, placing them ½ inch apart. Fold on the pulled thread lines and stitch three ⅛-inch pin tucks. Roll the edge of the smaller skirt sections and whip to the free edge of the lace beading on the upper sec-

tions. Feather Stitch along the rolled edge. Measure down from the rolled edge ¾ inch and pull a thread for a tuck. Pull threads for two more tucks, placing the first ½ inch below the pulled line and the second ½ inch below the last. Stitch the three tucks. Work a row of Feather Stitches along the rolled edge.

ASSEMBLY

Roll and gather the skirt tops to fit the yokes. Whip to the entredeux on the yokes, folding the back yoke facings and continuous lap to make a standard back opening.

Gather the sleeves between the dots, using small running stitches. Distribute the gathers across the top of the sleeve and baste it to the armhole. French seam.

Seam skirt side seam and sleeve in one operation, using a French seam.

RUFFLE

Join the ruffle pieces with French seams to form a circle. Roll and whip one side, attaching a lace insertion. Whip a lace edging to the insertion, gathering the lace very slightly—it should be just full enough to flare, not to gather. With a single strand of embroidery floss, work a row of Feather Stitches along the rolled edge.

Roll the top edge of the ruffle and gather it to fit the bottom of the dress. Whip entredeux to the gathered ruffle. Roll the bottom edge of the skirt and whip it to the entredeux at the top of the ruffle.

NECK EDGE FINISH

The neckline is to be finished with a row of entredeux and a gathered lace edging. There are two methods by which this finish can be accomplished.

The first is carefully to roll the neck edge and whip the entredeux to it, as has been done in the rest of the dress. Care must be taken not to stretch the fabric in this method.

An easier method of applying the entredeux without changing the neckline by stretching it is to sew it to the neck edge either by hand or machine before trimming away the batiste edge. Stitch the entredeux to the right side of the yoke, stitching as close as possible to the ridge of the entredeux. Trim away all but ⅛ inch of the seam allowance of the yoke. Roll the batiste edge of the entredeux over the trimmed seam allowance and whip it in place. Make the stitches into the seam allowance and not into the yoke itself so none are visible on the right side.

Cut away the remaining edge of the batiste on the entredeux, gather the lace edging, and attach to it.

Make three handmade buttonholes in the yoke. Sew on buttons. Insert ribbon in beading in the skirt.

SLIP

MATERIALS
Batiste, white, ½ yard
Lace insertion, ¼ inch wide, 1½ yards
Lace edging, ½ inch wide, 2½ yards
Buttons, baby-size, white, 2
Embroidery floss, white, ¼ skein

INSTRUCTIONS
Cut yokes following the slashed lines on the dress patterns. Cut two skirt pieces 8½ × 22½ inches. As always, cut all the pieces on lines marked by pulled threads.

French-seam front and back yoke pieces are joined at the shoulders. Roll the bottom edges of the yoke pieces and whip to entredeux. With a single strand of embroidery floss, work a row of Feather Stitches just above the rolled edge. Turn back the back facings and press; roll and whip the edges of the facings to hem.

Cut out armholes in the skirt sections as for the dress. Finish the top of the skirt back with a placket, as for the dress.

French seam the side seams. Roll the bottom edge and whip a lace insertion to it. Whip a gathered lace edging to the insertion. Feather Stitch along the rolled edge.

Roll, whip, and gather the top edges of the skirt pieces to fit the yoke pieces. Whip to the entredeux on the yoke pieces, turning back the yoke facings and continuous laps.

Make the little scalloped edging for neck and armholes by turning a ⅛ inch hem and stitching with invisible stitches as for any hem. Create the scalloped effect by making every third stitch around the hem, knotting it, and pulling it tightly.

Make two handmade buttonholes in the yoke back. Sew on the buttons. Work a row of Feather Stitches along the neckline.

cut on line

top of skirt

side seam

Armhole Cutting Guide for Skirt

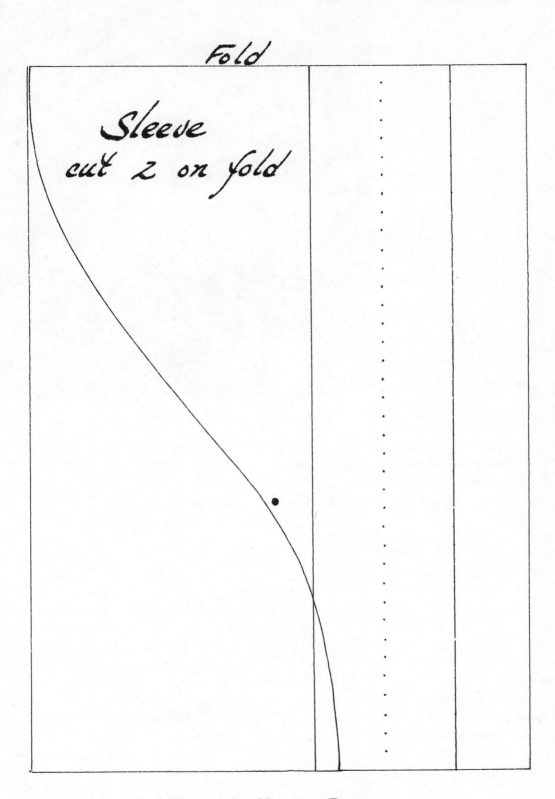

Fold

Sleeve
cut 2 on fold

PATTERN FOR HEIRLOOM DRESS

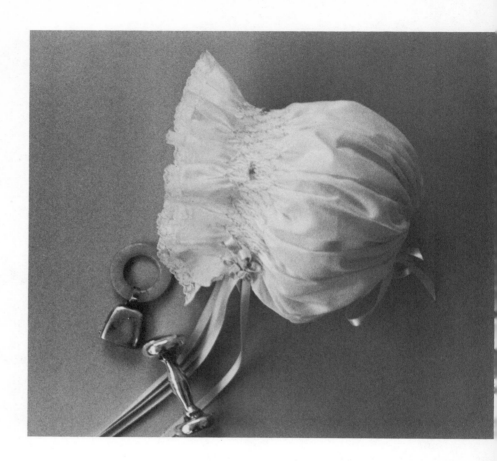

Smocked Bonnet

English smocking combines beautifully with Heirloom Sewing to make this delightfully feminine summer bonnet. The lace-edged ruffle is a perfect frame for a beautiful little face.

This is an easy project, made from a straight strip of fabric gathered with five rows of smocking and finished with ribbon ties.

SIZE
Six months and 1 year.

MATERIALS
Batiste, white, 45 inches wide, ¼ yard
Lace edging, ½ inch wide, 1¼ yards
Embroidery floss, pale pink, ½ skein
Ribbon, ¼ inch wide, pink double-faced, 2½ yards
Ribbon, ½ inch wide, pink double-faced, ¼ yard
Sewing thread, white cotton

INSTRUCTIONS
For 6 months size pull threads and cut the fabric to make a piece 8 × 45 inches. For 1 year size, cut the piece 9 inches wide.

English smocking is worked over gathering threads which form the pleats. The easiest way to establish the gathers is to take the cut fabric to a smocking shop and have it machine-pleated with five rows of gathers placed so that the first row is 1 inch from the front edge.

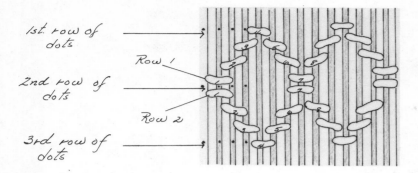

1st row of dots

Row 1

2nd row of dots

Row 2

3rd row of dots

DIAGRAM FOR SMOCKING

The alternative is to purchase smocking dots in a package and transfer five rows to the bonnet, placing them so the first row is 1 inch from the front edge.

Before beginning to smock, roll, whip, and attach ungathered lace edging to the front edge.

If you are using dots, run a gathering thread down each row of dots, picking up each dot with the needle. With either kind of gathering, pull up the threads so the gathered strip measures 12 inches (12½ inches for a one-year-old).

Using three strands of embroidery floss, work the lattice-pattern smocking. Beginning at the left side, work a cable stitch on the second row of dots, then a two-step wave upward to the first row of dots making stitches 2 and 3 as shown in the diagram. Stitch 4 is another cable on row 1. Work a two-step wave back down to the second row of dots and make a cable stitch, stitch 7. Continue thus across the row. Row 2 is worked in reverse to create the diamond pattern. Work two more rows to complete the pattern.

Work three Bullion Stitch rosebuds (style 2 on page 144) into the center row of smocking diamonds. Place one at the top center of the bonnet; place the other two halfway between the top center and the side edge.

Remove the gathering threads. Roll and whip the side edges to hem. At the back edge turn a hem ½ inch wide to the inside and stitch it in place, leaving the ends open as for a casing.

Thread ½ yard of the ¼-inch ribbon through the casing and pull it up tightly. Tie the ribbon ends in a bow.

Cut the remaining ¼-inch ribbon into two 1-yard pieces. Fold each piece in half—the looped end will be the tie end. Turn back 2 inches of each of the two cut ends. Holding them together, stitch back and forth through them and gather them tightly about 1 inch from the fold. Tack to the bonnet at the sides.

Cut the ¼ yard of ½ inch ribbon into two equal pieces and make a ribbon rosebud from each. Tack the rosebuds over the gathered loops of the ribbon ties.

SMOCKED BONNET

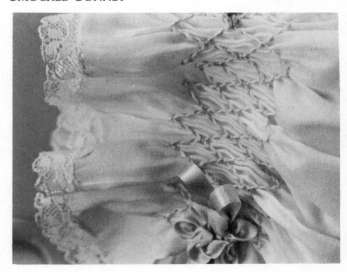

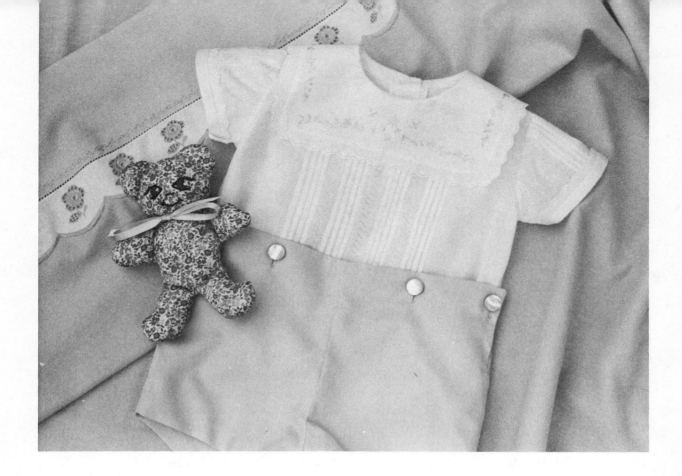

Sunday Suit I

A little boy needs a very special outfit just as much as a little girl does, and here it is—an old-fashioned button-on suit with a hand-sewn shirt that is delicate and elegant without being one bit "sissy." The pants and embroidery are a pale shade of blue, the shirt white, hand-tucked, and featuring a square bib-shaped collar.

Although the shirt is entirely handmade, the sewing techniques used are not those requiring all cotton, so the outfit can be made of easy-care fabrics. The result will be just as pretty as if all cotton were used and the benefits of the blended fabric add to the usefulness of the suit.

SIZE
Six months

MATERIALS
Broadcloth, 45 inches wide, pale blue, ⅝ yard
Batiste, 45 inches wide, white, ⅝ yard
Embroidered batiste edging, ½ inch wide, 1½ yards
Buttons, white pearl, ½ inch diameter, 6
Buttons, white pearl, ¼ inch diameter, 5
Embroidery floss, pale blue, 1 skein
Snaps, 3
Sewing thread, white and pale blue

26

INSTRUCTIONS

The seam allowance for all pieces is ¼ inch. Follow the diagrams, cutting on the solid lines and sewing on the dotted lines.

Using tissue or tracing paper, make a pattern for each piece of the suit by tracing the drawing given for it. Note that the pieces for the pants back are too large for a complete diagram to fit on a single page of this book. The part of the diagram which would have extended beyond the page edge is shown inside the larger piece. Trace the larger section first, marking the small dots at the ends of the cutting lines. Next, move the paper so that the dots starting the lines of the remaining section are on top of the dots you marked at the end of the first section. Note that the slashed line of the new section is now where the slashed line of the old section was. Now trace the balance of the piece.

Even though it is not necessary to use all-cotton fabric for the shirt, it is best to use the Heirloom Sewing methods of construction (see pages 124–25). Instead of immediately cutting out the shirt pieces on the cutting lines, begin working each piece while it is still part of the rectangle of fabric of the dimensions noted on the pattern, so that tucks can be marked with a pulled thread.

SLEEVE

Start with a 4 × 11-inch rectangle for each sleeve. Mark the center of the 11-inch side. On each side of the center, measure out ½ inch and mark four tucks spaced ½ inch apart. Pull threads and sew ⅛ inch pin tucks following the directions for Heirloom tucks on page 125. With a single strand of embroidery floss, work a line of Feather Stitches down the center of the space between the two groups of tucks. Press tucks away from the center.

Center the sleeve pattern on the tucked fabric and use a washable fabric pen to mark the cutting line. Reinforce the stitching of the tucks where they cross the cutting line. Cut out the sleeves.

With the right sides together, sew the top edges of two of the cuff pieces together, joining in the embroidered edging. Trim the seam. Turn. Press. Position the cuff at the lower edge of the right side of the sleeve. Sew only the cuff facing to the sleeve. Trim the seam. Press seam upward toward the sleeve. Turn up the unfinished cut edge and hem it in place, covering the seam.

Repeat for the other sleeve.

SHIRT FRONT

Begin with a rectangle 19 inches wide and 14 inches long. Mark the center of the 19-inch side. On each side of the center, measure out ½ inch and mark four tucks ½ inch apart. Skip 1 inch and mark another group of four tucks, also ½ inch apart. Pull threads to mark the tucks, and sew ⅛ inch pin tucks.

With a single strand of embroidery floss, work three rows of Feather Stitches down the center of the 1-inch spaces between the groups of tucks. Press tucks away from the center.

Place the pattern for the shirt front over the tucked piece, matching the centers. With a washable fabric pen, mark the cutting line. Reinforce the stitching at the neck and shoulders where the tucks will be cut and then cut the shaping.

Sew the front to the back at the shoulders,

making a French seam. Gather the sleeves between darts and pull up just enough to fit the armhole. Again using a French seam, sew in the sleeves. Sew underarm and sleeve seams also using a French seam. Make a narrow hem in the back facing edges.

COLLAR

Cut out the pieces marked Collar I and transfer the embroidery design to the front, placing it as shown on the pattern piece. With a single strand of floss, embroider the garlands. Use Outline Stitch for the stems, French Knots for the flower centers, Lazy Daisy for those flower petals which are shown as straight lines, and Satin Stitch for the other flower petals and leaves.

With right sides together, sew the outer edge of the collar to the collar facing, inserting embroidered batiste edging in the seam and mitering the front corners neatly. Trim the seam; turn; press. Using a narrow bias strip, attach the collar to the neckline, turning back the back facings on the lines indicated.

Turn up a ¾-inch hem at the bottom edge of the shirt. Work five buttonholes to fit the ¼-inch buttons, evenly spaced down the left back. Sew on the buttons.

PANTS

Cut the pants and lining as directed on the pattern pieces. These may be assembled on the sewing machine and plain seams used since the pants are lined.

Stitch the center front and back seams of both pants and lining. Clip the curves. Make the darts in back of both. Press the seams and darts.

With the right sides together, stitch front to back at the sides from the small square (■) marked on the back pattern to the bottom edge. Clip the seam to the square. Repeat for the lining.

With the right sides together, slip the lining into the pants. Stitch the tops together, beginning at the square on the front side and stitching up the side of the placket, across the top, and down the other placket to the square. Repeat for the back, stitching around the placket extensions and again stitching from square to square. Trim corners; press seam. Turn pants right side out.

Joining the lining to the pants at the leg edges is a bit tricky. Leave the pants rightside-out. Turn one leg so that the right sides are together at the leg edge. Stitch from crotch to the side seam. Repeat for the other side of the leg. Repeat for the other leg. Press the pants and turn ½ inch to the inside at the crotch. Slip stitch to close. Sew three snaps to the crotch extension.

Make eight buttonholes to fit the ½-inch buttons. Work two on pants front, two on pants back, and one on each side of each side placket and extension. Sew the buttons onto the shirt in the proper position. (If desired, use a small square of batiste under each button as a reinforcement.)

SUNDAY SUIT I, DETAIL SHOWING SHIRT CONSTRUCTION AND EMBROIDERY.

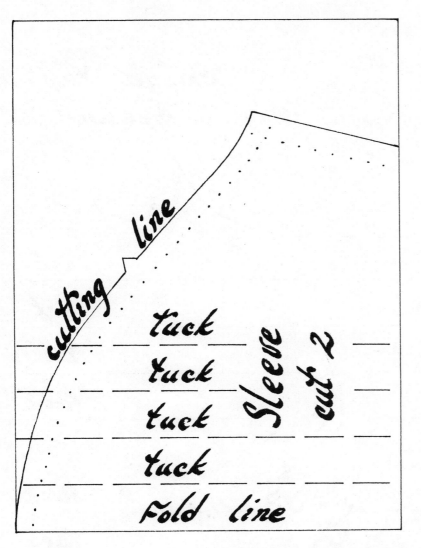

tuck

tuck

tuck

tuck

Sleeve cut 2

cutting line

Fold line

cutting line

Cuff cut 4

Fold

PATTERN FOR SUNDAY SUIT

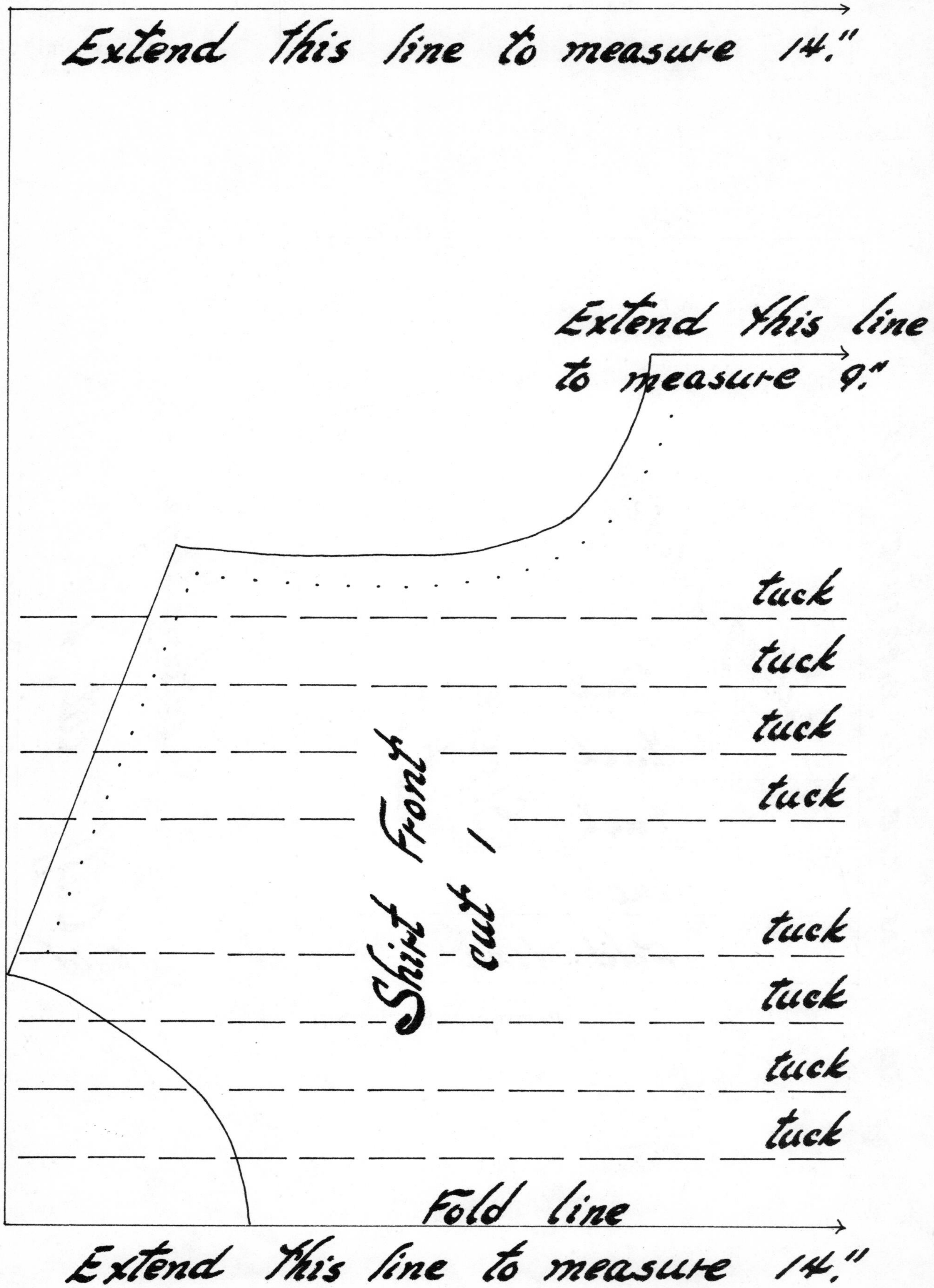

Extend this line to measure 14."

Extend this line to measure 9."

tuck

tuck

tuck

tuck

Shirt Front
cut 1

tuck

tuck

tuck

tuck

Fold line

Extend this line to measure 14."

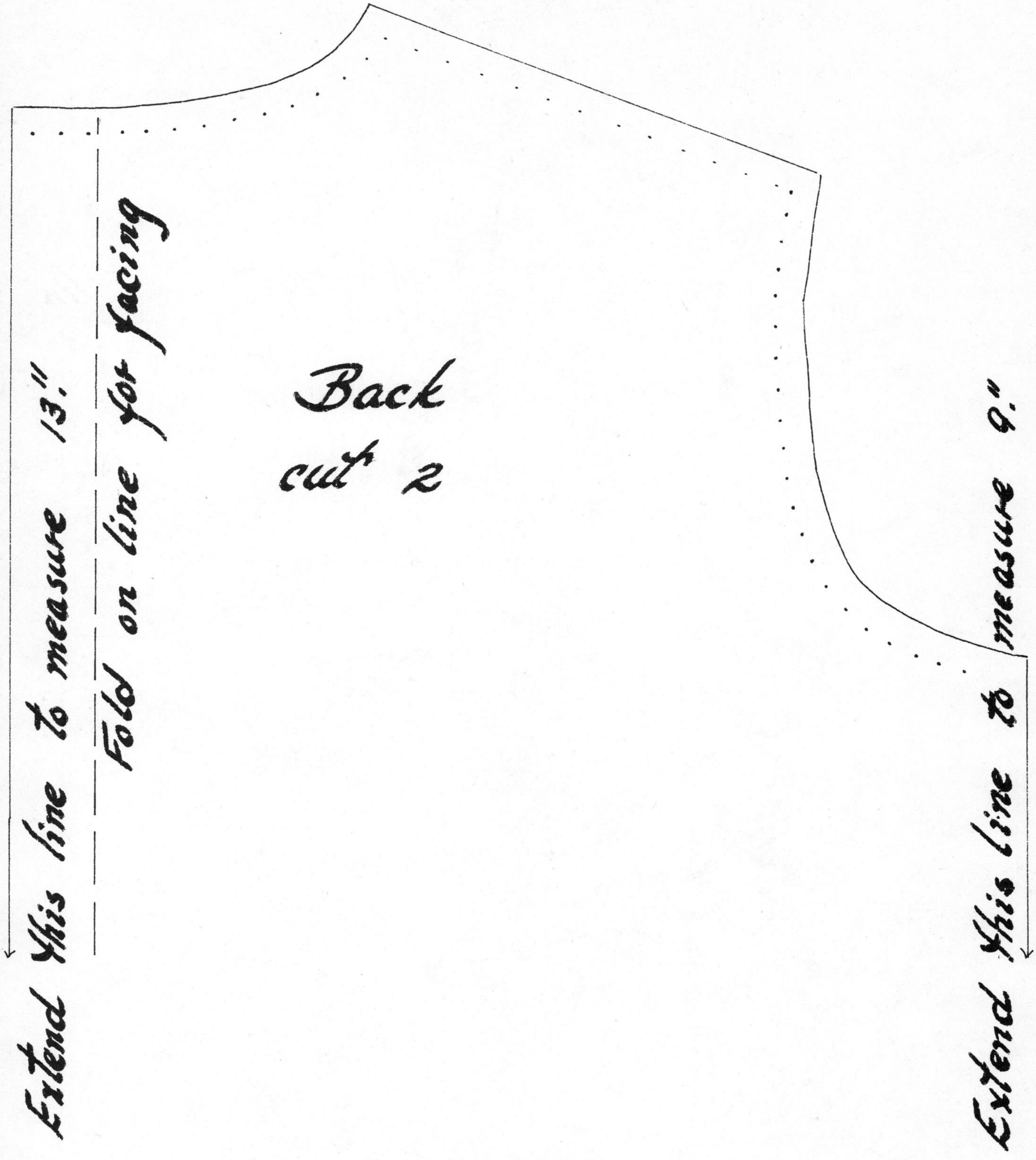

Back
cut 2

Extend this line to measure 13."

Fold on line for facing

Extend this line to measure 9."

PATTERN FOR SUNDAY SUIT

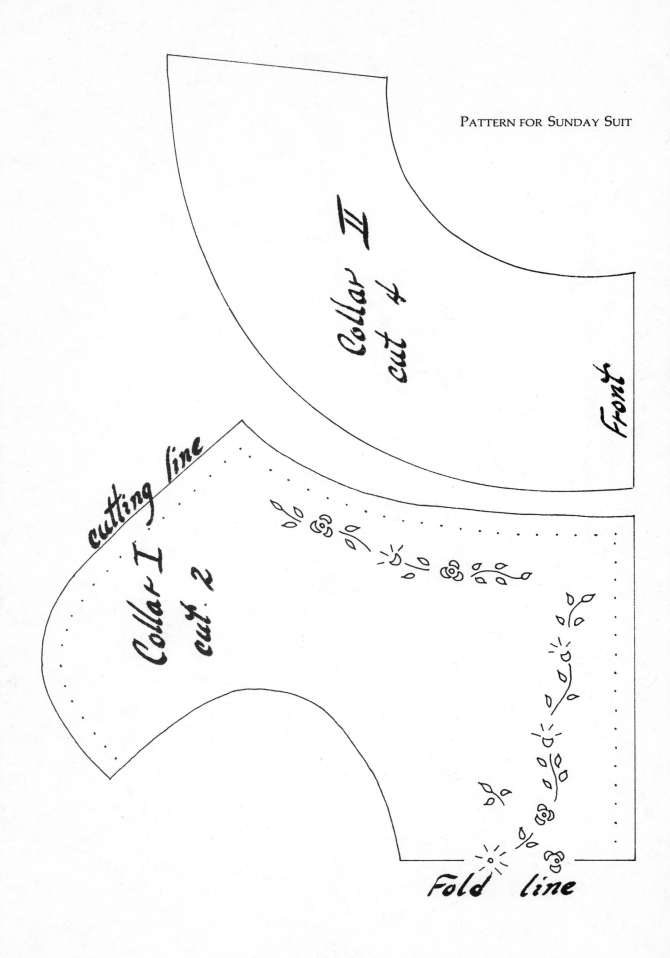

Collar II
cut 4

Front

cutting line

Collar I
cut 2

Fold line

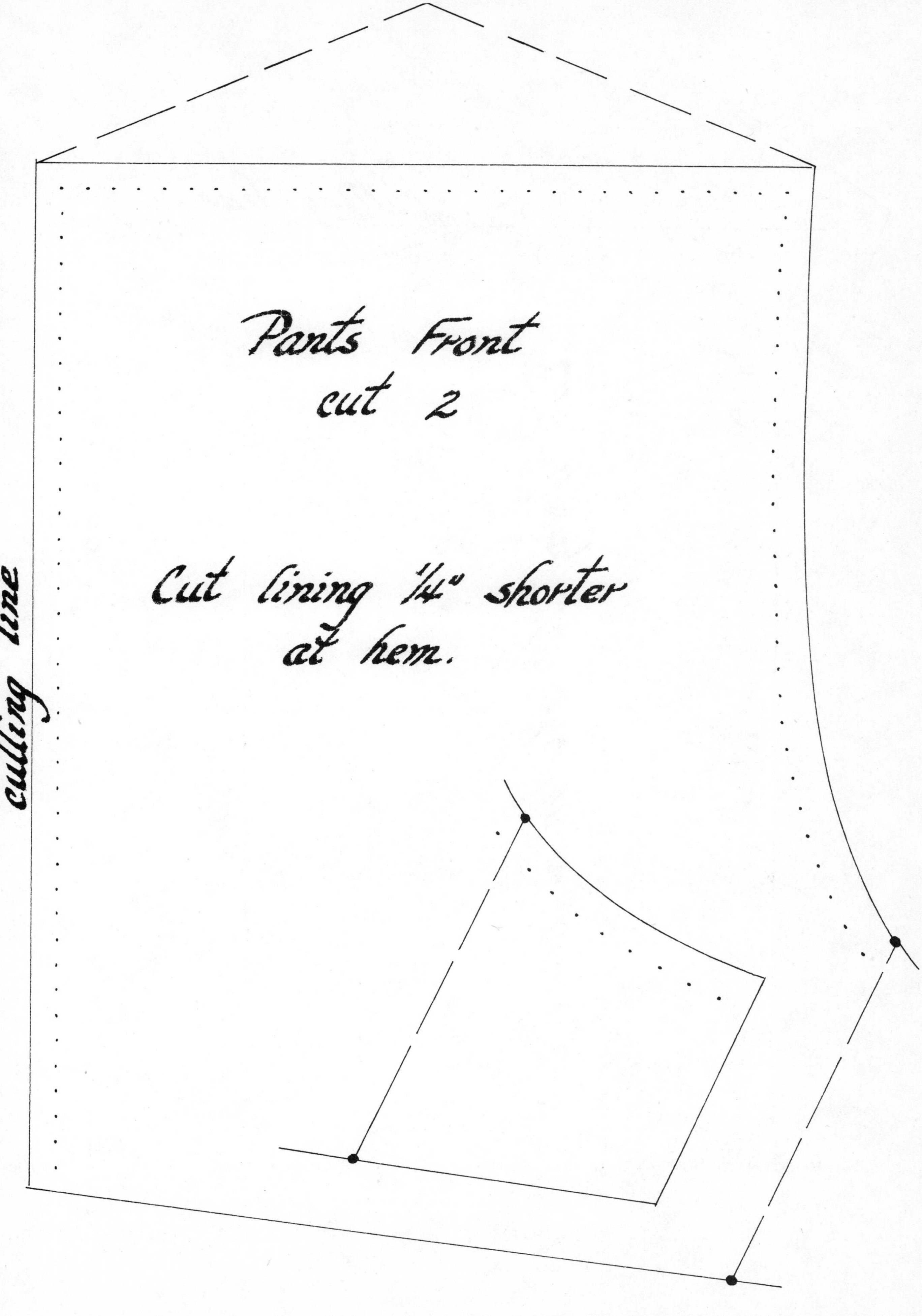

Pants Front
cut 2

Cut lining ¼" shorter
at hem.

cutting line

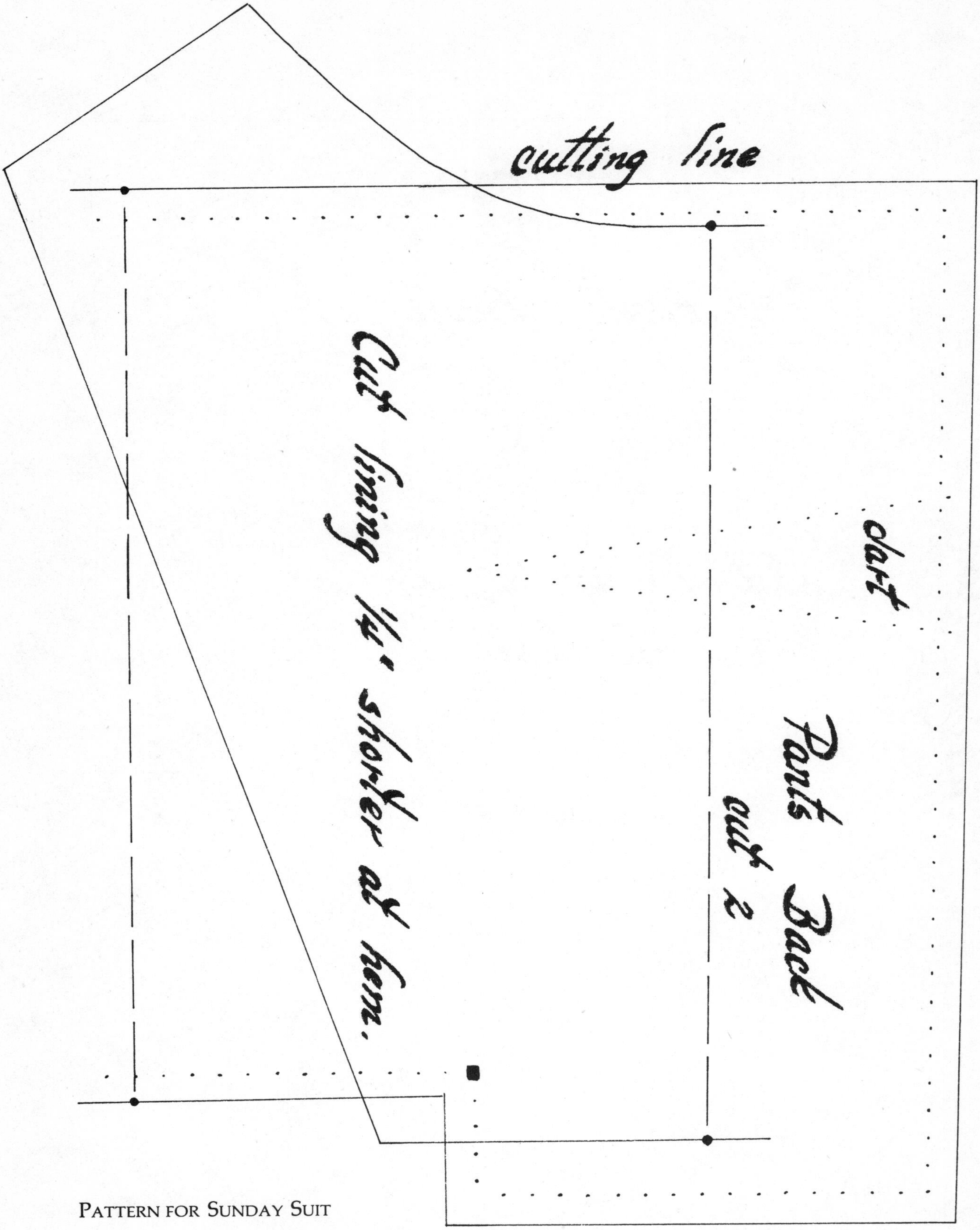

cutting line

Cut lining 1/4" shorter at hem.

dart

Pants Back
cut 2

PATTERN FOR SUNDAY SUIT

Sunday Suit II

Commercial pattern designers virtually ignore little boys when assembling their collections of attractive clothes, but once you have started Heirloom Sewing, the lack of commercial patterns will not be a problem. Slight alterations in the basic pattern for Sunday Suit I make Sunday Suit II different but still delicate and dressy. Embroidered trim, entredeux, and a total of sixteen tiny whipped tucks embellish the shirt front. A small Peter Pan collar and short sleeves finished to match complete the cute shirt. The addition of the shaped front changes the pants just a little bit.

SIZE
Six months

MATERIALS
Broadcloth, 45 inches wide, pale yellow, ⅝ yard
Batiste, 45 inches wide, 100 percent cotton, white, ⅝ yard
Embroidered batiste insertion, 1 inch wide, ¾ yard
Embroidered batiste edging, ½ inch wide, 2 yards
Entredeux, white, 2⅝ yards
Buttons, white pearl, ½ inch diameter, 6
Buttons, white pearl, ¼ inch diameter, 5
Sewing thread, white and yellow
Snaps, 3

INSTRUCTIONS

This version of the suit uses the basic pattern pieces of Sunday Suit I with several small alterations. The pants front is cut on the slashed line creating the points; the collar is the Peter Pan collar marked Collar II.

The seam allowance for all pieces is ¼ inch. Follow the diagrams, cutting on the solid lines and sewing on the dotted lines.

Using tissue or tracing paper, make a pattern for each piece of the suit by tracing the drawings given. Once again, the diagrams for large pieces are telescoped; follow the directions given at the start of the instructions for Sunday Suit I to transfer the complete outline to your fabric.

When making the pattern for the front of the pants, cut the top on the slashed line forming the points at the top.

When making the fabric rectangles for the pattern pieces, use pulled threads to make the cutting lines as described in directions for Heirloom Sewing on pages 124–25. The fabric rectangles for the shirt back are the same as those for Sunday Suit I. The rectangles for the shirt front and sleeves are cut as follows:

Shirt front, 15 × 14 inches

Sleeves, 2 pieces, 9½ × 4½ inches

Use basic Heirloom construction methods in making the shirt—working first on the rectangles of fabric, then cutting to the pattern outline after all embellishment is complete.

SHIRT FRONT

Begin with the 15 × 14-inch rectangle. Fold the 15-inch side in half and mark the center. Pull a thread and cut the piece in half down the center. Roll and whip one 14-inch edge, attaching entredeux. Roll one edge of embroidered batiste insertion and whip it to the entredeux. Roll the other edge of the trim and whip it to another strip of entredeux. Roll the edge of the other shirt-front section and whip it to the entredeux.

Measure out from the entredeux ¼ inch and pull a thread to mark a tuck. Pull threads for seven more tucks ⅜ inch apart. Pull threads for eight corresponding tucks on the other side of the shirt front. Fold on the marked lines and make whipped tucks following instructions for Heirloom tucks on page 125. Press the shirt front well. Cut out to match the shirt front pattern, reinforcing the tucks at shoulder and neck where they cross the cutting line.

SLEEVES

Begin with one of the 9½ × 4½-inch rectangles. Fold the long side in half, mark the center, and pull a thread. Cut the piece in half. Following the procedure for the front, insert a band of the embroidered trim and entredeux. Measuring as for the front, pull threads and make six whipped tucks on each side of the embroidered panel.

Reinforce the tucks where they will cross the cutting line; press well; cut out the sleeve.

Cut the long side of the cuffs on the fold of fabric rather than as shown on the pattern—eliminate the ¼-inch seam allowance. Stitch one side of the cuff to the right side of the sleeve. Trim the seam. Turn the raw edge of the cuff back and hem over the seam.

Whip a row of entredeux to the edge of the cuff. Roll, whip, and gather the embroidered edging to fit the entredeux. Whip to the entredeux. Turn up the cuff. Tack the edging to the seam to hold it in place.

Repeat for the other sleeve.

COLLAR

Mark the front edges of the four collar pieces as noted on the diagrams. Trim away from the front edges of the two top pieces a strip ¼ inch narrower than the embroidered trim. Roll the trimmed edge of the collar and attach entredeux. Roll the edge of the embroidered trim and whip it to the entredeux. The top collar pieces should now be the same size and shape as the originals.

Join the collars to the facings. Trim the seams. Turn. Whip a row of entredeux to the outside edges. Roll, whip, and gather the embroidered edging to fit the collars. Whip to the entredeux.

SHIRT BACK

Roll and whip the edges of the back facings to hem. Mark the fold line. Press.

SHIRT ASSEMBLY

All seams are to be French seams.

Sew front to backs at the shoulders.

Gather the sleeves between the dots. Pull up gathers to fit the armholes. Sew in the sleeves. Sew the sleeve underarm and side seams in one operation.

Attach the collar to the neckline with a narrow bias strip, turning back the facings at the same time.

Turn up a ¾-inch hem around shirt bottom and stitch. Make five buttonholes evenly spaced down the left back. Sew on the buttons.

PANTS

Construct the pants as explained in the instructions for Sunday Suit I, adding points to the front top as shown. Make buttonholes in the pants, placing them as for the first suit (the front two centered at the top of the points).

Slip the shirt into the pants. Mark the positions for the buttons and sew them on. (To avoid tearing the shirt under the buttons, either reinforce the shirt under each button with a square of fabric or sew a small button to the back of each button.)

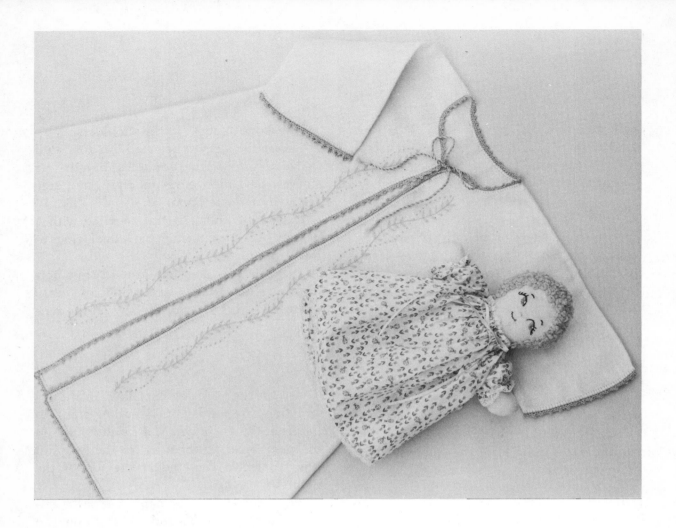

Embroidered Flannel Kimono

There's nothing more practical and pleasing than a flannel kimono—seems like babies have always worn them for exactly those reasons. This simple and timeless garment is comfortable for a summer morning or snuggly warm for after-bath. Make several in a palette of colors—trim some simply with a Blanket-Stitched edge and embroider one or two just for fun. Cut at the line shown in the diagram for a shorter version, and make several from a cool fabric for baby to wear in hot weather with his fancy diaper covers.

(The short pattern may also be used to fashion the Quilted Sacque shown on page 42.)

Lovely flannel now comes in either 100 percent cotton or in an easy-care of cotton and synthetic which is just as soft. The latter is my choice since I feel that whenever possible clothes for a baby should require little care. The use of cotton embroidery floss for both the crocheted edge and the embroidered garland make this a garment that will come out of the dryer ready to be used.

SIZE
Infant

MATERIALS
White flannel, 45 inches wide, ¾ yard
DMC embroidery floss #3325, light blue, 5
   skeins
Steel crochet hook, size 8
Sewing thread, white

INSTRUCTIONS
The pattern shown must be enlarged. Make a grid of 1-inch squares on a 14 × 24-inch sheet of graph paper; draw the pattern on your grid, following the smaller original, square for square. The shape is simple and does not require great drawing skill to copy, but you may use a commercial pattern if you prefer and trim it as shown.

Use the enlarged pattern for cutting both the back and the fronts of the kimono. Draw both the back and front necklines on the pattern piece. Cut the back first, placing the fold line of the pattern on the fold of the fabric and using the marked back neckline. Then cut two front pieces using the lower neckline.

Using a sewing machine, work a row of zigzag stitching in matching thread around the entire outside edges of all pieces.

All seam allowances are ¼ inch. Sew back to front at the shoulders and side seams. Press the seams open. Carefully trim the seams to the zigzag stitching.

Rolling the zigzag stitching to the wrong side, hem all edges with Buttonhole Stitching worked with two strands of the blue embroidery floss.

Separate a full skein of embroidery floss into three two-ply threads. (Ask someone to help you with this so you can avoid cutting the floss and have the full 8-yard length to use to work the crocheted edge.)

Using the two strands of embroidery floss and working into the loops of the Buttonhole Stitch, work a row of single crochet around all the edges of the kimono. (You may, if you wish, omit the Buttonhole Stitching and simply crochet over the hem edge, eliminating one step, but the effect will be slightly heavier than shown in the photograph of the finished kimono.)

Join the beginning and end of the single crochet round with a slip stitch. *Work three single crochet in the next three loops; chain three, single crochet in same loop*—picot formed. Repeat the steps described between *'s around the entire garment. Finish the sleeve edges in the same manner.

Copy the embroidery design to make a transfer pattern. Four repeats of the design will reach from the neck edge to the hem as shown on the photographed model. You can add another repeat to turn the corner at the neck, or you can repeat the design all the way around the hem of the kimono if you are ambitious.

Transfer the embroidery design to the front of the kimono and, using two strands of floss, embroider in the stitches indicated on the drawing.

From a full six-ply strand of the blue floss, cut a 2-yard length. Following the instructions on page 131, make a pair of Bishop Cord Ties and attach the two to the neck edge of the kimono as shown. Tie in a bow.

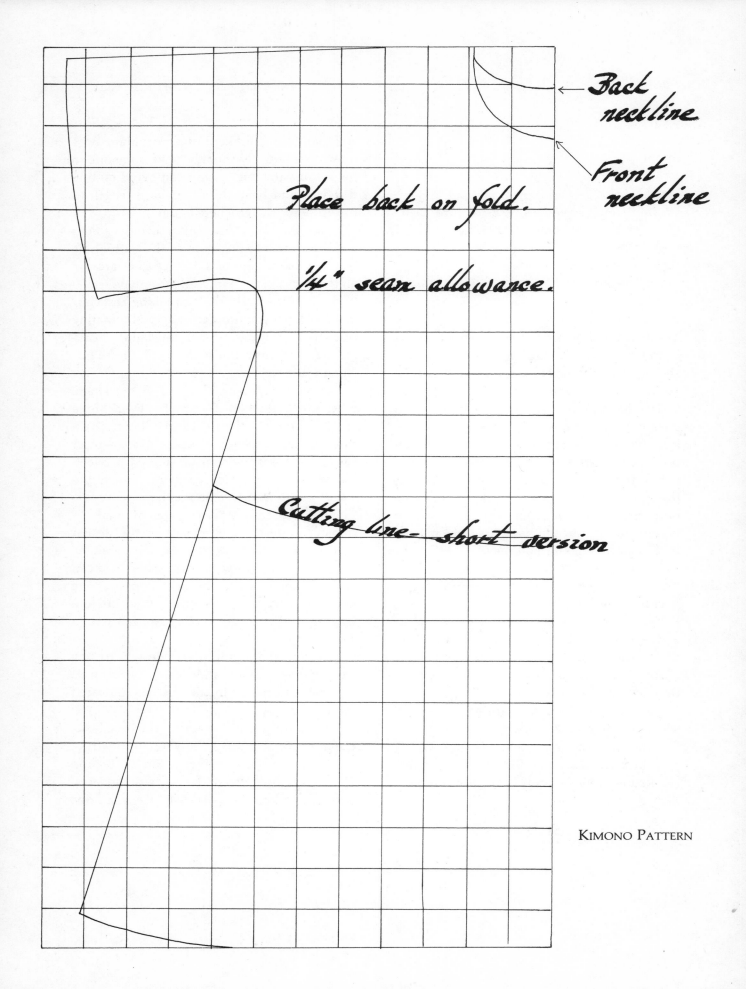

Back
neckline

Front
neckline

Place back on fold.

¼" seam allowance.

Cutting line— short version

Kimono Pattern

KIMONO EMBROIDERY MOTIF

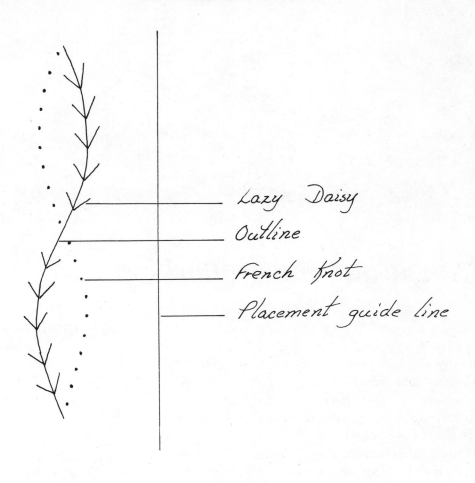

Lazy Daisy

Outline

French Knot

Placement guide line

Quilted Sacque and Bonnet Set

This outfit, like many little girls who would be happy to wear it, appears fragile and delicate but actually will outperform more utilitarian-looking versions. Since it is made of a silky polyester fabric that goes into the washer and dryer without needing touch-up ironing, it is always ready to wear. The use of synthetic quilt filler makes it puffy and luxurious. Dainty-looking quilting and Feather Stitching add trim that is feminine but practical.

If your baby hasn't arrived yet and you want to be sure the outfit can be used by either a girl or a boy, make it in white, blue, or yellow rather than the pink specified, with or without the lace edging. It will still be luxurious and pretty but not quite so obviously feminine.

SACQUE

SIZE
Infant

MATERIALS
Polyester fabric, pink, 45 inches wide, 1 yard
Polyester quilt filler, 22 × 28 inches
White embroidery floss, 1 skein
Ribbon, pink, ½ inch wide, 2½ yards
White lace edging, nylon, ½ inch wide, 5 yards
Sewing thread, pink

INSTRUCTIONS
Use the short version of the pattern for the Embroidered Flannel Kimono on page 38, enlarging the pattern as noted in the kimono

instructions and making the following adaptation. Eliminate the seam allowance on the shoulder edge and place the shoulder on the fold of the paper so you cut a paper pattern with an outline like that shown in the small drawing of the sacque. (Note that the slope of the shoulder for the sacque will be slightly different than for the kimono.)

Placing the back on the fold line, cut two complete sacques—one for the outer layer, one for the lining. Cut the quilt filler interlining with the same pattern.

Baste the quilt filler to the wrong side of one piece. (Baste all outside edges and run a few rows of basting vertically through the garment to keep it from shifting during construction.)

With the right sides together, baste the sacque to the lining. Stitch, leaving an 8-inch opening for turning at the back hemline. Trim the seam to ⅛ inch. Trim away excess quilt filler in the seam allowance; clip the curves at the underarms and neck. Trim the corners closely.

Turn. Slip-stitch the opening to close. Baste around the entire edge to hold the seam line in place.

Measure in from the sleeve hem ⅜ inch and run a row of quilting stitches along that line. Measure in from the quilting row ½ inch and make another row of quilting. Work a third row of quilting ⅜ inch from the last.

With a single strand of white embroidery floss, work a row of Feather Stitches down the middle of the ½-inch space between the first two quilting rows. Repeat on the other sleeve edge.

With the right sides together and using a small whipping stitch, sew the underarm and sleeve seams. Quilt and Feather Stitch the entire edge of the sacque—around the neck, down the fronts, and around the hem—to match the sleeves. Gather the lace and whip to the complete outside edges of the sacque and sleeves. Make ribbon rosettes following the direction on page 127 and attach ribbon ties to the neck.

BONNET

Following the drawing, make a paper pattern for the cap and crown pieces. Cut two of each from the pink fabric—one for the cap and one for its lining. Cut one from each pattern for the quilt filler interlining.

Baste the quilt filler to the wrong side of one cap piece and one crown piece. As with the sacque, run a few rows of basting through the body of the piece so there will be no shifting during construction.

For both cap and lining, sew the back seams. Trim excess filler from the seam allowance. Press the seams open. Gather both on the gathering line indicated on the pattern. Sew the cap pieces to the crowns.

With the right sides together, slip the bonnet into the lining and sew them together, leaving a 3-inch opening for turning at the center back. Trim the seam. Turn. Slip-stitch the opening to close.

Quilt around the entire bonnet, placing the row ⅜ inch from the edge. At the front edge, work two more rows of quilting and a row of Feather Stitches to match the finish on the sacque. Finish the front edge with a gathered lace edging. Make ribbon rosettes following the directions on page 127, and attach ribbon ties to each side of the cap.

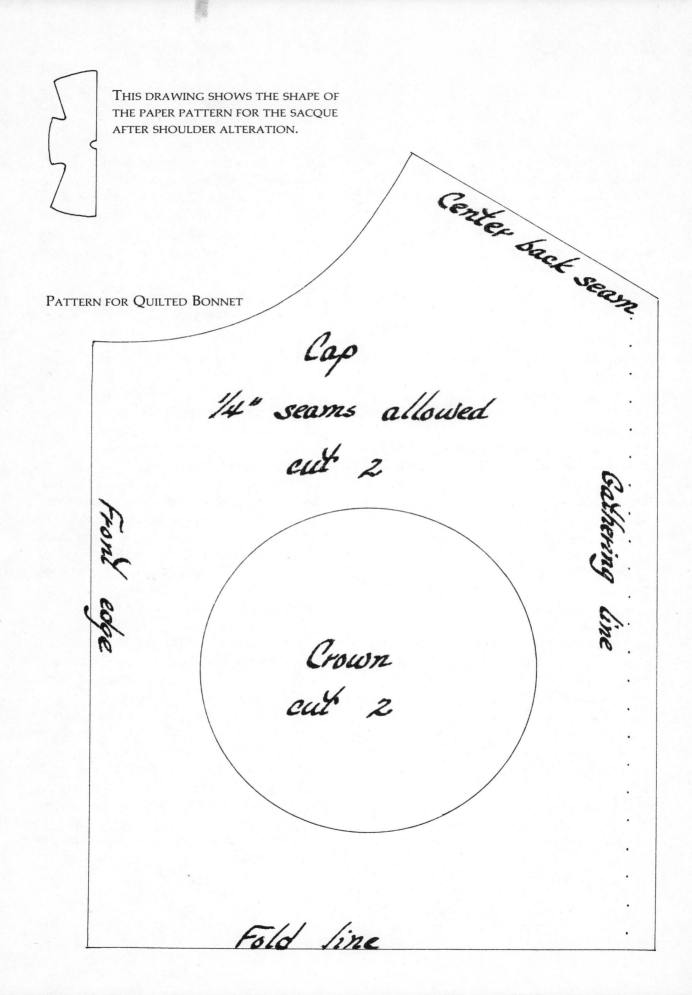

THIS DRAWING SHOWS THE SHAPE OF
THE PAPER PATTERN FOR THE SACQUE
AFTER SHOULDER ALTERATION.

PATTERN FOR QUILTED BONNET

Center back seam.

Cap

¼" seams allowed

cut 2

Crown

cut 2

Front edge

Gathering line

Fold line

Christening Blanket or Shawl

For ages the most elegant christening accessories have been white, and many of us are strongly inclined to uphold that tradition today. Gradually, however, we are seeing the introduction of color into the clothing used for this precious ceremony. In reflection of this trend, but wishing to maintain a delicate feeling, I decided to use the palest of pastels to embroider the garland of this blanket.

I was sitting in the garden room lacing the pale blue ribbon through the hemstitched border, thinking how bold I had been, when a dear friend dropped in with her daughter and month-old grandson. The new mother was "wearing" her baby in a blue denim pouch which hung from her shoulders. He was curled against her, sleeping as happily as if he were at home in his own bed. When she took him out to introduce him, I could not help smiling at his untraditional—to me, at least—clothing. He was wearing an indigo blue denim diaper cover styled like jeans with a famous designer's name on the pocket. Topping that was a short smocklike shirt made of a bright yellow, red, and green peasant-print fabric. His booties were designed to look like jogging shoes!

He opened his eyes as I held him, stretched, and tried to smile even though his nap had been interrupted, and in that brief moment he reinforced my belief that it really does not matter what a baby wears so long as it is comfortable, clean, and easy for the mother to maintain. Little David was as miraculous in his modern attire as he would have been in a hand-stitched day gown. No

45

change of clothing could alter the fact that he was a very special little boy!

We always seem to gravitate to the kitchen or the garden room in this house, and so when we had settled in the garden room where I had been sewing, my friend and her daughter admired my work while I admired baby David. After dutifully inspecting the stitching and commenting on the fabric and design of the piece, this young mother reflected that she might like to make one herself as a gift for one of her contemporaries, changing the background color to yellow and embroidering with the brightest peasant colors.

How appalling, the traditionalist in me reacted, but the idea nevertheless captured my interest as a designer and I later worked a small swatch on a scrap of yellow wool. In-

stead of my pastels, I used bright primary colors and laced a royal blue ribbon through the hemstitched border. The result was indeed attractive and I pinned a label to the edge reading "David's Christening Blanket." It would take a lot more than color to outshine little David!

Here, then, is my version of the christening blanket for you to adapt as you please. Make it as suggested in white with pale colored embroidery and palest blue ribbon interlacing the hemstitching, or work it entirely in pure white—the texture of the stitches and the gleam of white satin ribbon will make it elegant and truly traditional. Or make David's blanket with brightest color and joyous abandon. Any of the three is certain to be a very special gift.

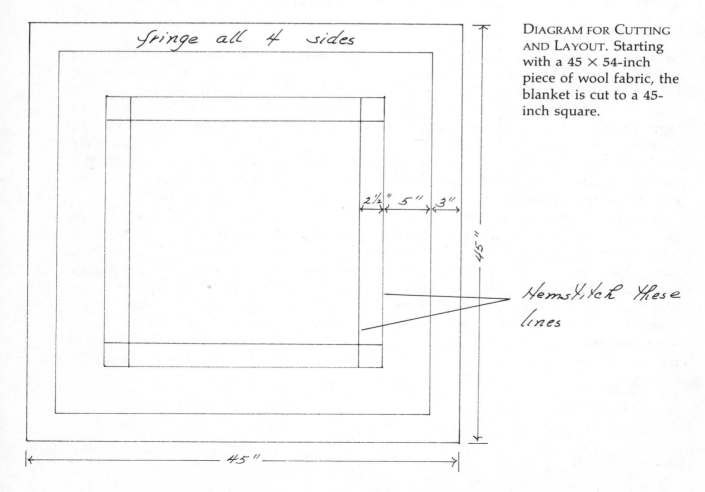

DIAGRAM FOR CUTTING AND LAYOUT. Starting with a 45 × 54-inch piece of wool fabric, the blanket is cut to a 45-inch square.

CHRISTENING BLANKET, DETAIL.

SIZE
39 inches square, exclusive of fringe

MATERIALS
Wool fabric, white, 54 inches wide, 1¼ yards
Crewel yarn as follows: B42, Whisper Blue, 9
   yards; 26P, Cloud Pink, 10 yards; 468,
   Yellow White, 10 yards; 537, Iced Mint, 9
   yards
Cotton thread for hemstitching
Ribbon, ⅛ inch wide, pale blue, 6½ yards
White silk or soft white batiste, 45 inches
   wide, ⅓ yard

INSTRUCTIONS
Choose a very soft white wool or wool-blend
fabric with a fairly open weave since threads
are to be drawn for hemstitching and fring-
ing. The one used for the photographed
model was a basket weave with about twenty

threads to the inch. (If using a fabric with
fewer threads to the inch, tie the fringe in
correspondingly smaller groups. Also, with-
draw fewer threads to make a channel to use
with the ⅛-inch ribbon when preparing for
hemstitching. If the thread count is greater,
use larger numbers of threads.)

Pulling threads to make certain it is perfectly straight, trim the fabric to a 45-inch
square. Make a fringe 3 inches wide on all
four sides by removing the cross threads. Tie
the thread ends in groups of six into over-
hand knots, pulling the knots up tightly
against the woven edge.

Measure in 5 inches from the fringed
edges and pull threads to mark the hemstitching pattern, as shown on the layout
diagram. Pull enough threads to make an
open channel about ⅛ inch wide. Hemstitch
both edges of each row. Tie together enough

threads in each group to make a square opening. (As noted above this may vary, but about six should be right.)

The diagram of the border motif is full size and shows the exact size and placement of the stitches used. The pattern for the border embroidery shows the skeleton needed for the transfer. Trace this pattern and transfer it down the center of the panels using the dotted center line as a guide for placing the design. Repeat as many times as necessary to cover the length of the panels.

The diagram of the corner motif is also full size and shows the stitches used. As in the garland, it is not necessary to trace the rosebud and leaves at the sides of the bow. It will be sufficient to trace just the flower centers and fill in the balance freehand.

Using the stitches and colors indicated on the diagrams, embroider all borders and corners referring if you wish to style I of the Embroidered Rosebuds on page 144 for more detailed help with the rosebuds. Press or block if necessary. Insert the ribbon in the hemstitched channels. Cut the ribbon rather than trying to turn the corners. Tack the ends lightly.

Even the most skillful of embroiderers will finish with a blanket that has an obvious wrong side, but both sides will be seen when the blanket is used. To make a prettier finish, I cut the silk into 3-inch strips, fold back ½-inch hems, and whip the strips to the wrong side of the embroidered panels. A pale blue Feather Stitch worked with a single strand of embroidery floss finishes this soft lining, which should also be applied to the little corner squares.

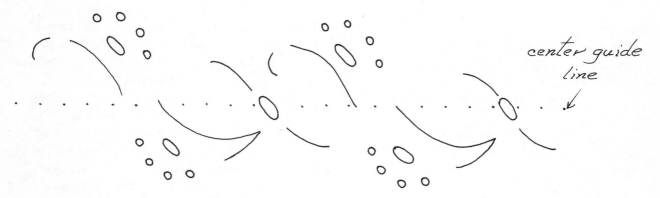

center guide line

PATTERN FOR BORDER EMBROIDERY. This skeleton of the embroidery pattern is all that is necessary to be transferred to the fabric. The less transfer color you put on the blanket now, the less you will have to worry about covering or removing later. Trace the design and stamp it as many times as necessary to reach from end to end of each panel. The lines shown are to be worked in Coral Stitch, the small dots are for French Knots, the large ovals are the rosebud centers, to be worked in Satin Stitch as described in Style 1, page 144.

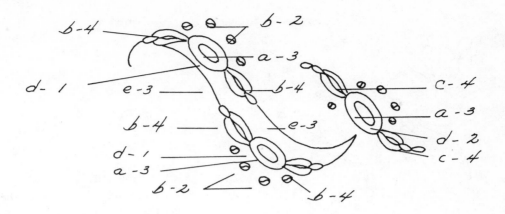

BORDER MOTIF. This sketch shows one full-size repeat of the border motif as it will appear after embroidery. Make your stitches just about the size shown and place them on the skeleton transfer as they are shown here. Note that there are two extra little stitches at the ends of the Lazy Daisy leaves on the single rosebud. These are to extend the curved line to a more pleasing end.

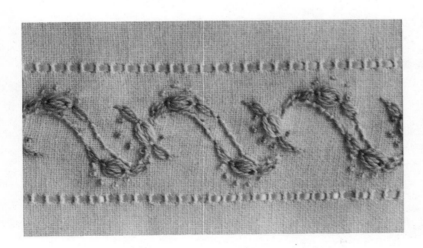

CHRISTENING BLANKET, DETAIL
SHOWING BORDER EMBROIDERY.

STITCHES

a — Satin
b — French knot
c — Lazy Daisy
d — Easy Rosebud
e — Coral

COLORS

1 — B42, Baby Blue
2 — 26P, Baby Pink
3 — 468, Baby Yellow
4 — 537, Baby Green

CORNER MOTIF. Trace and transfer this motif to each of the four corner squares. Use the dotted outline as a guide for placing the motif within the squares.

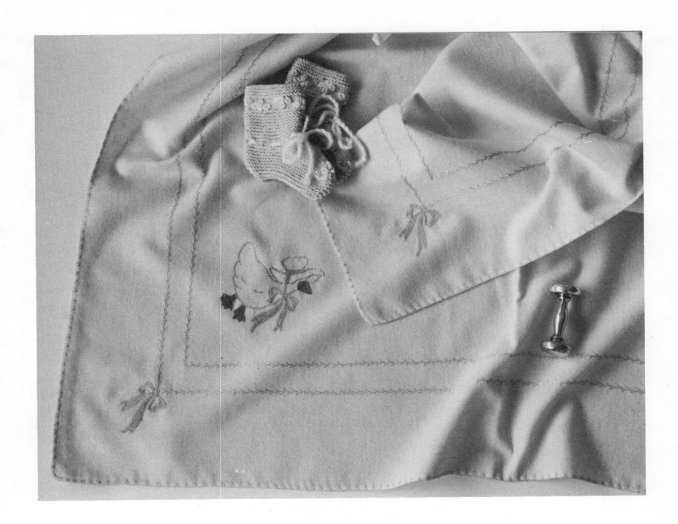

Receiving Blankets

Fashions in baby clothing and infant care have changed just as much as customs in the adult world. Time was when lots and lots of soft receiving blankets were a necessity. Now that a baby wears cute little knitted suits that provide protection from chin to toes, only a few wrappings are needed. But these practical, small blankets are still useful and very important in the early days of a baby's life, so it is wise to make several.

They are easily made and can be embel-lished with whimsical embroidery or simply trimmed with a Blanket Stitch hem. You'll be surprised to find that you can whip up three for the price of buying one and the big bonus will be that yours will be softer and prettier.

MOTHER GOOSE BLANKET

SIZE
45 × 45 inches

MATERIALS

Flannel, yellow, 45 inches wide, 1¼ yards
Cotton embroidery floss: About ½ skein
  each: pale blue, white, orange, yellow, and
  pink
Sewing thread, yellow

INSTRUCTIONS

Flannel is available in both 100 percent cotton and in a blend of cotton and polyester. Price and quality are about the same. The choice is personal.

Trim the edges of the fabric to straighten. Run a row of zigzag stitching around all four edges, staying as close as possible to the edge. Turn a single-fold hem the width of the stitching to the wrong side and press. With three strands of embroidery floss, work a row of Blanket Stitches around all four sides to finish the hem.

Measure in from the hem 4 inches and mark a line for the first row of Feather Stitches. (I do not actually mark, but fold the fabric and press to make a guideline on which I stitch.)

Mark another line 1 inch inside the first. On the first line work a row of blue Feather Stitches. On the inside row, use pink floss. Use three strands of floss for each.

Trace the motif for Mother Goose and transfer it to one corner of the blanket, positioning it as shown in the photograph. Work entirely in Split Stitch with three strands of embroidery floss in the colors noted on the diagram. Make the feet, ribbons, and bill solid, using close rows of stitches. Work other details in a single outline.

Transfer only the bow from the motif to each corner of the blue Feather Stitch row. Work it in solid blue Split Stitch as in the Mother Goose motif.

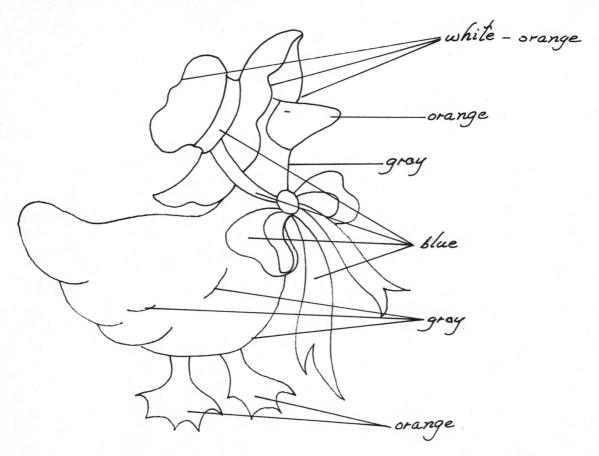

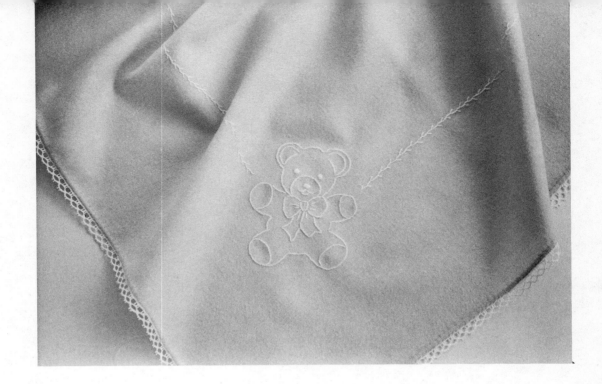

TEDDY BEAR BLANKET

SIZE
45 × 45 inches

MATERIALS
Flannel, blue, 45 inches wide, 1¼ yards
Cotton embroidery floss, white, 1 skein
Cotton lace, white, ¼ inch wide, 5 yards
Sewing thread, blue

INSTRUCTIONS
Look for a fairly heavy cotton lace edging that resembles tatting or crochet (as shown in the photograph).

Trim the fabric to straighten. Turn back a very narrow hem and stitch by hand. Whip the lace edging to the outside edge of the hem.

Measure in 5 inches from the hemmed edge and mark a line for Feather Stitching. (If you prefer, fold the fabric and press to make a guideline rather than actually marking the blanket.) Trace the Teddy Bear motif used on the bib on page 58 and transfer it to the blanket, placing it on one corner, as shown in the photograph. With three strands of white embroidery floss and Split Stitch, work the bear. Use Satin Stitch for the eyes and nose.

With three strands of embroidery floss, work a row of Feather Stitches around the blanket on the marked line. Begin and end the line about ½ inch from the bear.

RIBBON GARLAND BLANKET

SIZE
45 × 45 inches

MATERIALS
Flannel, white, 45 inches wide; 1¼ yards
Brazilian embroidery floss: variegated pale pink, 5 skeins; variegated pale blue and pale green, 1 skein each
Steel crochet hook, size 8
Sewing thread, white

INSTRUCTIONS

Brazilian embroidery floss is a shiny rayon thread that comes in 24-meter skeins. It has a luxuriously soft look but is washable.

Trim the fabric to straighten. With a sewing machine, work a row of zigzag stitching around all four sides, staying as close as possible to the edge. Turn a single-fold hem the width of the stitching to the wrong side and press.

Open a skein of the pink floss and unwind it so you have the full length with which to work. It will be easier to handle if you wind it around a card to keep it from tangling.

Holding the folded hem in place, work a row of single crochet around the entire blanket with the pink floss. Join the beginning and end of the single crochet round with a slip stitch. *Work three single crochet in the next three loops; chain three, single crochet in the same loop—picot formed. Repeat the steps described between *'s around the blanket.

Measure in from the hem and mark a line for Feather Stitching. (If you prefer, fold the fabric and press to make a guideline rather than actually marking the blanket.) Trace the hearts-and-bow motif used on the bib on page 59. Cut the hearts and leaf sprigs on each side of the bow apart from the transfer. Place the bow and heart beneath it on one corner of the line marked for the Feather Stitching so the knot of the bow is exactly on the corner of the line as shown in the photograph. Place the cut-out hearts and leaf sprigs so they are spaced as in the original but parallel to the marked line. Trace the single heart and its leaf sprigs and transfer it to each of the other three corners.

With a single strand of the pink thread, work a row of Feather Stitches on the marked line, beginning and ending always just short of the embroidery motifs as shown in the photograph.

Using single strands of floss, embroider the balance of the design. Use blue Split Stitch for the hearts, pink Satin Stitch for the bow, green Outline and Lazy Daisy for the leaf sprigs.

Flannel Sheets

Flannel top sheets are a luxury you can give a baby only if you make them, for as far as I know they are not available in stores. Plain percale top sheets can be found, but few if any have fancy trim or embroidery.

The idea for these sheets came to me when I began sewing two receiving blankets together to make a sheet large enough to fit a crib and realized that with 45-inch wide fabric I could make soft warm sheets that fit the crib perfectly. Flannel had been a wonderful fabric for receiving blankets so I choose it for my homemade sheets. They are warm in winter and often provide just enough warmth during a summer night in an air-conditioned room.

Elaborate instructions are not necessary. Start with a 1¾-yard length of 45-inch flannel and use your imagination. The two pictured here have 4-inch hems which were decoratively hemstitched at the local smocking shop for a very nominal fee. The blue one has no other adornment.

The yellow sheet has had a border of very pretty Swiss embroidered eyelet sewn just below the hemstitching. A row of yellow Feather Stitches along the lower edge of the hem finishes the sheet.

Plain hems will be pretty too. Allow at least 4 inches for the hem as this looks very tailored. Trim the hem with several rows of Feather Stitching or use one of the embroidery patterns designed for other projects and apply it just below the hem. You might want to embroider the baby's monogram on the hem, or you may just want to stitch up several perfectly plain sheets. They are certain to be used and appreciated and everyone will wonder why they didn't think of this simple and useful bedding themselves.

Quilted Bibs

Bibs are easy to make and every baby needs lots of them, but this is not why they were included in the book—it was the price and poor quality of ready-mades. Half a yard of quilted fabric and a package of bias binding will make several plain bibs that can be trimmed with lace, embroidery, or ruffles to far outshine any that can be purchased.

Easy-to-sew ready-quilted fabrics make this a very practical project since the finished bibs are not only much prettier than bought ones, they also function just as well. Choose the quilted fabric in baby pastels, bright primaries, endearing baby prints, bright calicos, or classic ginghams. Some quilted fabrics are double faced—both sides are finished—while others have only a nylon knit protecting the interlining. Either is appropriate; two pieces will be needed if the fabric has just one finished side, but the end result is a bib which is a little thicker and thus nicer.

If you choose the single-faced fabric, ½

yard will make two bibs. Simply cut two pieces and join the two with bias binding. Sew the first strip of binding around the outside edge, beginning and ending at the shoulder neck edge. Sew another strip of binding to the neck edge, letting it extend about 9 inches at each side to form ties. To trim with a gathered eyelet ruffle, sew the ruffle to the right side of one piece, then join the two pieces right sides together in a seam, leaving the neck edge open for turning. Trim the corners and turn. Bind the neck edge with bias tape.

To make a bib from double-faced fabric, simply cut one piece, finish the edges with bias binding tape, and trim as desired. With this kind of fabric, ½ yard will make four bibs.

The yellow bib shown in the photograph was cut from the double-faced fabric, bound with a red and green plaid bias binding, and trimmed with the Teddy Bear motif worked in Outline Stitch in two shades of brown with a bright red bow.

The pink bib with gathered eyelet trim was made from single-faced quilted fabric. The embroidery was worked before the bib was constructed—a nice plus. The motif was embroidered as follows: the bow is pale blue Satin Stitch; leaf sprigs are Lazy Daisy and Outline Stitch in light green; hearts are filled with Trellis Couching and outlined in medium pink. The eyelet was gathered and inserted in the seam as described above. The neck edge was bound with bias tape which was extended to make ties.

The other pink little girl's bib was also made from the single-faced fabric and embroidered entirely in white Outline and Satin Stitch. The full motif shown was placed just below the neck edge, and the little sprig noted on the diagram was repeated at the bottom of the bib on the curve at each side. The embroidery was completed, then the two pieces were joined with white bias binding. Half-inch wide nylon lace was then gathered and whipped to the outside edge of the binding. About 2 yards of lace were used and the embroidery was worked with less than half a skein of floss.

The cheerful clown-faced bib pictured was cut from two layers of single-faced quilted fabric which were bound together with extra-wide bias tape having a bright printed pattern. The color on the clown's face is fabric paint; the design is merely outlined with three strands of embroidery floss and Outline Stitch.

Fabric paints or dyes are a quick way to get a lot of color. They dry quickly and can be applied with ordinary water-color brushes. Several brands are available. New types of crayons will accomplish the same effect. The design outline is traced on paper, then colored in with the crayons and transferred to the fabric with a hot iron. The color is warranted to be permanent. Fabric markers can be used for similar effects, but check the labels to make certain the markers are made for fabric or they will bleed. Acryllic paints are not appropriate as they would make the bib shed liquids and lose its effectiveness as a bib.

If you wish, the color can be left off and the clown face just outlined in color. You'll have a bright, happy-faced bib.

Bib

Extend space between
dots to measure 8¼."

Center Front
Place this line on fold

Embroidery Motifs for Bibs

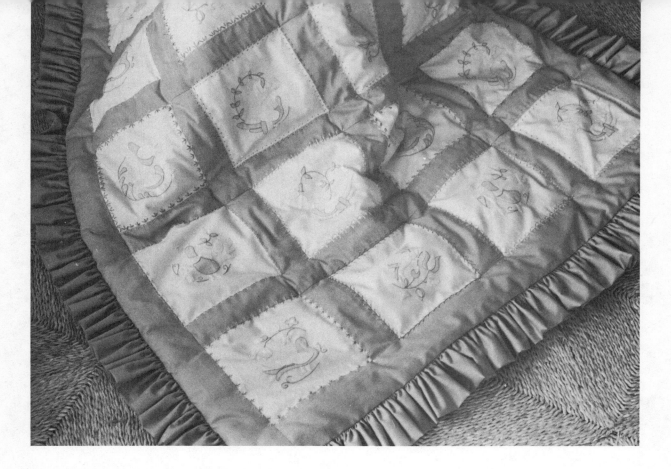

Shadow-Embroidered Comforter

Picture a nursery decorated around this soft comforter and the pillows that accompany it—wallpaper in a small blue-and-white country print, white or fruitwood furniture, and ruffled country curtains. It would be a peaceful and traditional room attuned to a baby's needs.

The mixture of pastel colors used for the embroidery makes it possible to change the blue background fabric to green, pink, or yellow to coordinate with another color scheme. The comforter's simplified adaptation of traditional pieced quilting techniques helps it fit in well with either contemporary or old-fashioned decorating plans. Crib bumpers covered in the same fabric as the comforter—with or without ruffles and embroidery—would be a nice way to finish dressing the bed.

Made of easy-care fabric, the comforter is practical for everyday use, soft, and very warm. The use of extra-puffy quilt filler makes it fluffy and pretty but not bulky or heavy.

Shadow embroidery is worked in the Herringbone Stitch on the wrong side of sheer or semisheer fabric. The result is a pale area of color showing through on the right side outlined by a row of small Back Stitches that appear to have been worked with a brighter shade of thread. The impression created is that a pale appliqué has been applied to the wrong side. This technique is often used on very expensive hand-embroidered table-cloths and on delicate handkerchiefs. Its soft appearance makes it very appropriate for baby things.*

SIZE
40 × 60 inches, excluding ruffle

MATERIALS
Broadcloth, 45 inches wide, pale blue, 5 yards
Batiste, 45 inches wide, white, 1¼ yards
Underlining fabric, 45 inches wide, white, 1¼ yards (this may be the same batiste as is used for the embroidered squares, or it may be a less expensive soft white fabric)
Quilt batting, crib size, super-lofty type
Cotton embroidery floss, DMC colors as follows: 3325, blue, 5 skeins; 726, yellow, 5 skeins; 954, green, 3 skeins; 894, pink, 5 skeins†
Sewing thread, white and pale blue

INSTRUCTIONS
Divide the white batiste into twenty-four 8-inch squares by pulling threads or measuring and marking carefully. (A well-made pieced quilt depends greatly on exact measuring and marking.) Leave the twenty-four in one large piece to embroider, or cut the batiste into smaller sections for easier handling.

Trace the six embroidery designs, center,

and transfer them to the squares. Transfer each design four times to produce a total of twenty-four.

Separate the embroidery floss and work all shadow work with two strands. Use two strands also for the Crazy Quilt patterns.

As noted, shadow work is ordinarily done from the wrong side of the fabric. It is predominantly Herringbone Stitch, but single lines as for a stem are worked in Back Stitch from the right side. Some stitchers, once they have mastered the Herringbone, prefer to work from the right side, feeling that this way they can more easily keep the little stitches on the right side more even. Whether you work from the right or wrong side, make certain that each area of the design is completely outlined by the Back Stitch.

Embroider all twenty-four squares, placing the colors as noted on the drawings of the motifs. If any traces of the transfer pencil show on the finished pieces, wash the squares to remove them before beginning assembly.

CUTTING
To make the comforter back, cut a rectangle measuring 41 × 61 inches. From the balance of the blue fabric cut the following pieces, using care to cut on the straight grain of the fabric to make putting the pieces together easier:

2 pieces, 4 × 61 inches
   (see *a* on the layout diagram)
2 pieces, 4 × 37 inches (*b*)
5 pieces, 3 × 37 inches (*c*)
18 pieces, 3 × 8 inches (*d*)

---

* *You might prefer to make one of the accompanying pillows—see page 68—before starting on the more complicated comforter, to get a better idea of the work involved and to see firsthand what the finished product will be like.*
† *NOTE: Since shadow work is done on the wrong side, the colors which show through to the right side will be paler than they appear in the skein. Keep this in mind if making color changes and work up a sample in your chosen colors to see how they will be affected by the working method.*

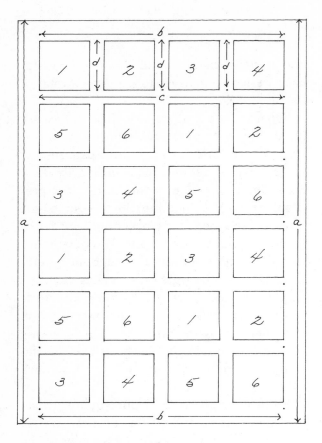

Enough 7-inch-wide strips to piece together
   a strip 14 yards long (to make the ruffle)
From white lining fabric cut twenty-four 8-
   inch squares.

LAYOUT
The diagram shows the placement of the
pieces. The numbers in the squares correspond to those on the drawings for the embroidery motifs. The letters key the fabric
pieces to those listed on page 61.

CONSTRUCTION
Pin or baste one lining piece to the back of
each embroidered square. Alternating the
embroidered squares with the 8-inch blue
strips (*d*), assemble six strips.

Join the six pieced strips to the five 3 ×
37-inch pieces (*c*) to make the center field.
Add the two 4 × 37-inch pieces (*b*) to the
field, one at the top and the other at the bottom. Finally, sew the two long side strips (*a*)
to the sides.

Press all the seams toward the blue fabric.

CRAZY QUILT EMBROIDERY
Embroider a Crazy Quilt design around each
square, working right over the seam and covering it. Six Crazy Quilt patterns are numbered to correspond to the six embroidery
motifs. If each pattern is used only with the
similarly numbered motif wherever it appears on the comforter, the distribution of
patterns will be even. Two extra Crazy Quilt
patterns, numbers 7 and 8, are included in
case you wish to vary the edging patterns.
Substitute them for two of the first ones or
use all eight, distributing them evenly.
Changing the arrangements of the colors on
an edging design each time it is used will
also make it seem that each square has a different edging.

Using two strands of embroidery floss,
work the designs directly over the seam,
shown as a dotted line on the left of each design in the diagram. First try the colors suggested in the instructions, then rearrange the
colors the next time the design appears to
create a different effect.

PATTERN 1
Outline the square with a row of pink Chain
Stitch worked directly over the seam. Make
the stitches about ⅛ inch long. From the

middle of each Chain Stitch, make a Straight Stitch ¼ inch long slanting out at about a 45 degree angle. Alternate these last stitches to slant first from one side, then the other, as shown in the drawing. Place a blue French Knot at the end of each slanting stitch.

PATTERN 2

Place a row of yellow French Knots on the seam, making the knots about ½ inch apart. With green floss, make long Straight Stitches lying on the seam and connecting the French Knots. Work a cluster of three Lazy Daisy stitches at each French Knot, placing the grouping as shown in the drawing. Alternate the clusters on the blue and white fabrics and use pink floss for those on the white, green for those on the adjoining blue.

PATTERN 3

Place a row of French Knots on the seam, making them about ½ inch apart. With pink floss, make two Lazy Daisy stitches perpendicular to the seam at each French Knot. Make a small Straight Stitch—about ⅛ inch long—on the blue side of the seam halfway between the Lazy Daisy stitches. Using blue thread, make a series of slanting stitches on the white side of the seam, placing them as shown in the drawing.

PATTERN 4

With yellow floss, work a row of Straight Stitches around the square, making the stitches ¼ inch long and placing them right on the seam. On the blue side of the seam, work clusters of three Straight Stitches placed in a fan shape at the end of every alternate yellow stitch. Using blue thread, repeat the clusters on the white fabric.

CRAZY QUILT EMBROIDERY PATTERNS. Victorian Crazy Quilts were adorned at every seam with fanciful combinations of easy embroidery stitches in a happy combination of wit and practicality that pulled the dozens of colors and fabrics into one. This group of patterns is to be embroidered on the seams of the Shadow-Embroidered Comforter and Pillows in much the same manner. Use just six or all eight and distribute them evenly over the blanket as suggested in the instructions.

PATTERN 5

With yellow thread, place a row of French Knots on the seam, making them about ½ inch apart. Using pink floss, make a fan-shaped cluster of three Lazy Daisy petals at

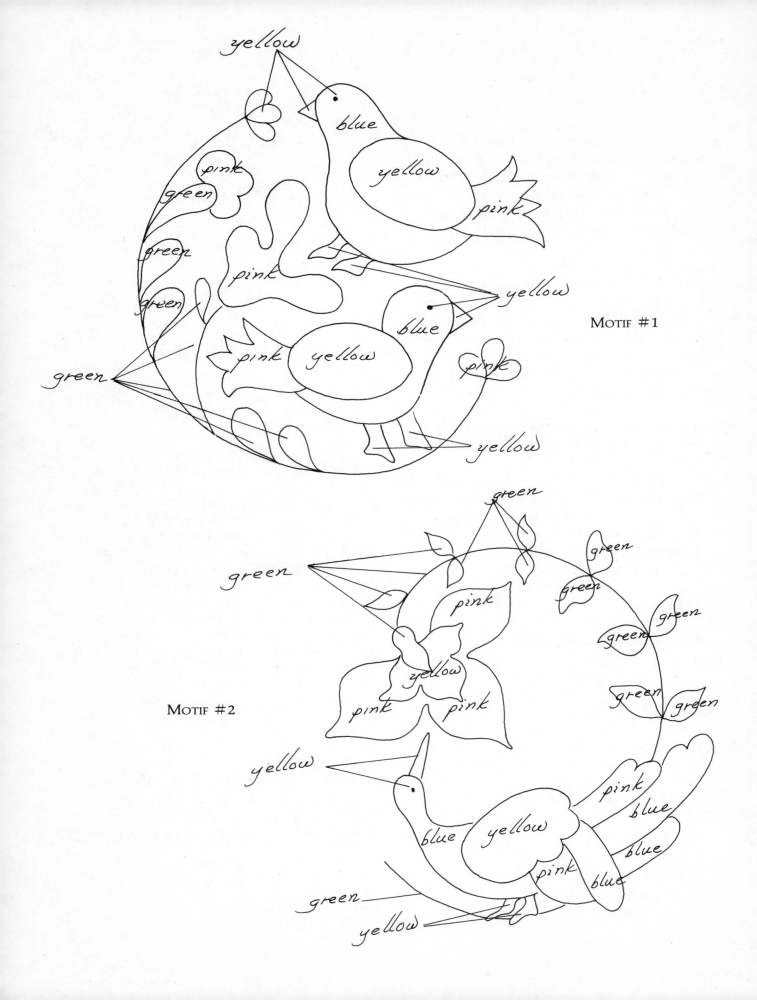

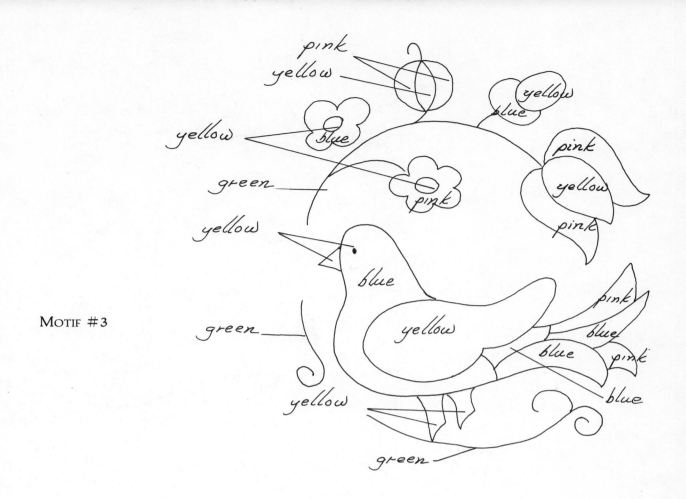

Motif #3

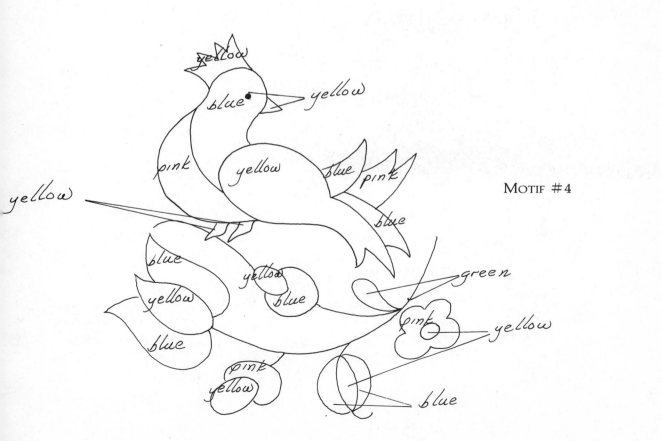

Motif #4

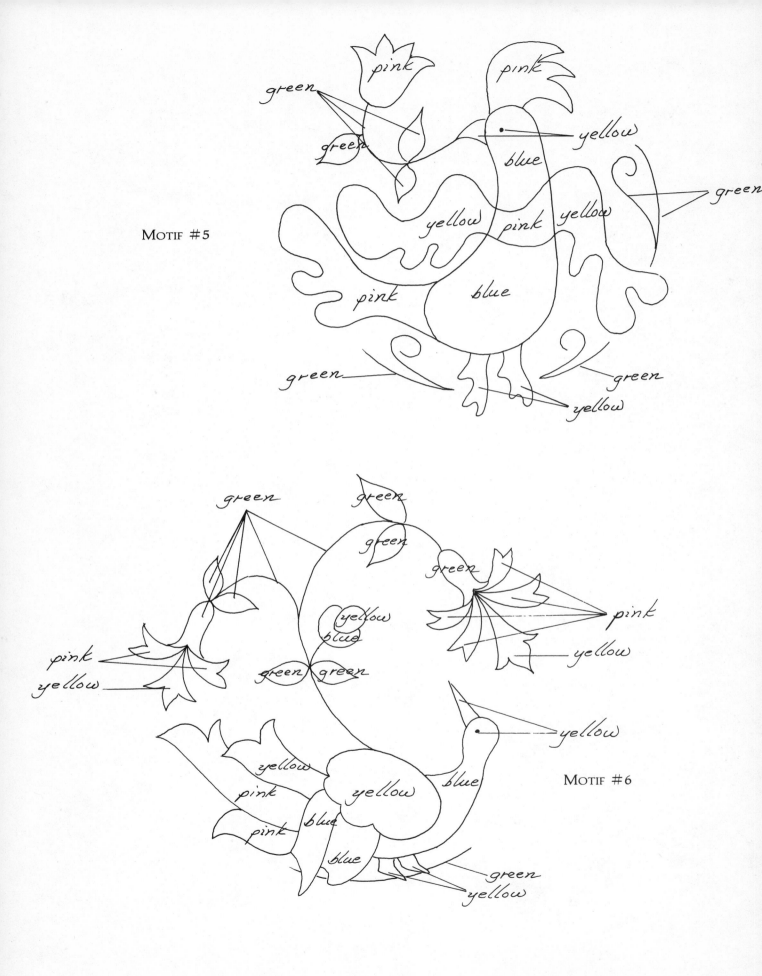

MOTIF #5

MOTIF #6

alternate French Knots on the white side of the seam. Place a single Lazy Daisy Stitch perpendicular to the seam at the other French Knots. Make a zigzag row of Straight Stitches as shown on the blue side of the seam.

PATTERN 6
Make a row of yellow French Knots on the seam, placing them about ½ inch apart. Connect the yellow dots with a line of green Straight Stitch also lying right on the seam line. With pink thread, make a Cross Stitch and a long vertical stitch centered over the green Straight Stitch. Also with pink, make a small horizontal stitch across the latter group of three stitches at the point at which they cross.

PATTERN 7
Work a row of pink Feather Stitches, centering it over the seam. On the blue side of the seam work a yellow French Knot at the end of each arm of the Feather Stitch. Make a yellow French Knot at the end of the stitches on the white fabric.

PATTERN 8
Center a row of blue Feather Stitches over the seam. Make a yellow Lazy Daisy Stitch over the arm of each Feather Stitch on the blue fabric. Repeat on the white side with green.

ASSEMBLY
Make the ruffle by joining the 7-inch-wide strips into one continuous piece 14 yards long. Join the ends. Fold the ruffle in half lengthwise to make a piece 3½ inches wide and baste the cut edges together. Gather at the basted edge to fit the quilt top.

Pin the ruffle to the right side of the quilt top, matching the raw edges. Allow extra fullness at the corners so the ruffle will lie flat. Baste in place with the longest stitch on the machine. With the right sides together, baste the quilt top to the back, joining in the ruffle. Seam, leaving the bottom open for turning.

Lay the quilt filler on top of the unturned quilt and baste it to the seam allowance with very long stitches. Turn the quilt. Close the bottom edge with invisible hand stitches.

Tuft the quilt at the corners of each embroidered square with three strands of blue embroidery floss. Do this by simply bringing the needle up from the back, leaving a 3-inch tail; making a small stitch, returning to the back, and tying the thread in a knot. Work both ends of the floss back into the quilt filler so they disappear.

The quilt pictured has the maker's name and the date embroidered in a single strand of blue floss in the lower left corner. It is very unobtrusive, but a very nice touch. Another possibility is to eliminate the bird pattern on one of the white squares and use the square instead to record the baby's name, birthdate, and your name. This makes a very personal gift and is a loving gesture for a special baby. Use your own script or the one included with the Ribbon-and-Toys Birth Record on page 86, and work in Back Stitch since it adapts so well to the curves of script.

Shadow-Embroidered Pillows

Designed and embroidered to match the Shadow-Embroidered Comforter (pages 60–67), these decorative pillows are pretty in a crib during the day; one provides a coordinating touch on a rocking chair and several can be used in a carriage. The pillows can be made as squares as pictured, or two motifs may be used to make an oblong shape.

SIZE

12 inches square, excluding the ruffle

MATERIALS

For each pillow:

Broadcloth, 45 inches wide, pale blue, 1 yard

White batiste, 1 8-inch square

White interlining, 1 8-inch square

Embroidery thread: colors as for the comforter (page 61), 1 skein each

Polyester fiberfill, slightly less than 1 pound

Sewing thread, white and pale blue

INSTRUCTIONS

Cut and embroider the white batiste square, following the instructions for the comforter. Use two strands of embroidery floss and stitches and colors as noted in the comforter motif diagrams.

CUTTING

From the blue fabric cut one 13-inch square for the pillow back, two pieces 3½ × 8 inches, and two pieces 3½ × 13 inches. From the remaining blue fabric cut enough 6½-inch wide strips to piece together a 3½-yard-long strip for the ruffle.

CONSTRUCTION

Baste the lining square to the wrong side of the embroidered square. Seam the two 8-inch strips to the sides of the square. Sew the two 13-inch strips to the top and bottom. Press the seams toward the blue fabric. Following instructions for the comforter, embroider one of the Crazy Quilt patterns around the square, working over the seam to cover it.

Seam the ruffle pieces to make one long strip. Join the ends to make a continuous piece. Fold in half lengthwise to make a 3¼-inch-wide double strip and baste the cut edges together. Gather the cut edges to fit the outside of the pillow top. Pin the ruffle to the right side of the pillow top, matching the raw edges. Allow extra fullness at the corners so the ruffle will lie flat. Baste in place. With the right sides together, sew the pillow top to the back, joining in the ruffle and leaving the bottom open for turning and stuffing. Clip the corners; turn. Fill evenly with fiberfill; close the seam with small, invisible hand stitches.

Gertrude Goose Wall Hanging

Today's nursery would not be complete without a graphic soft sculpture to brighten the walls and add a touch of whimsy. A trip through an infants' shop confirms this happy trend—cribs are decked out in fluffy comforters and bumpers, while matching pillows, diaper stackers, and soft wall hangings carry out a nursery theme. It adds up to a cheerful but expensive room.

Few of the decorative touches are hard to duplicate, but the wall hanging is the easiest one of all to adapt and make at home. Our baby's Gertrude Goose with her bunch of bright balloons is original, gay, and graphic. (Gertrude also appears on the Rainbow Comforter, page 75, if you want to carry out the theme.) Unlike hangings found in the stores, Gertrude has a skeleton of cardboard to give her body and slightly sharper lines, this being my own preference.

The basic plan for this project is a good starting point for your own original design or adaptation of a design. You can enlarge a figure from the nursery wallpaper or pick some cute animals from a child's coloring book or a favorite storybook. Paint or appliqué the details and construct your hanging in the manner outlined below to make a nursery decoration that is special to you.

70

SIZE

Goose is about 16 inches tall; balloons are 8 inches in diameter

MATERIALS

Broadcloth, 45 inches wide, ⅓ yard each: red, yellow, blue, green, orange, vivid pink, and purple

Broadcloth, 45 inches wide, white, ½ yard

Heavy cord or twine, 11 yards

Foam rubber, ½ inch thick, 36 inches wide, 1 yard

Posterboard or heavy cardboard, 36 inches square

Velcro fasteners, ½ inch size, 10

Thick craft glue

INSTRUCTIONS

Using an 8-inch plate as a pattern for the balloons, outline seven circles on the posterboard. Use the outline inset in the body pattern to add a knotted end to each balloon. Cut out the seven balloons.

Lay one of the posterboard balloons on each color fabric and trace an outline which is 1 inch larger than the posterboard on all sides.

Using the plate again, cut a circle from each color fabric—these will be the backing for the balloons. Trace the posterboard pattern on the foam and cut out seven balloons. Glue one foam cutout to each posterboard balloon.

Place one of the larger fabric balloons on top of the foam, pull it smoothly to the back, and glue it in place with thick craft glue. Pull the fabric to the back evenly so a smooth, rounded edge results on the front, but do not pull so tightly that the posterboard buckles.

Turn under ½ inch on the matching round

backing fabric and glue it over the raw edges on the back.

Cut the cord into seven equal pieces. Knot one around the extension of each balloon.

GOOSE

Make a tracing of the goose body by combining the sections. Transfer the pattern to posterboard and cut it out. Cut out the feet and bill pieces. Trace each piece on the foam and cut the pieces out.

Cut the foam for the feet and bill just to the dotted lines on the pattern pieces. Using the posterboard body, trace an outline 1 inch wider than the pattern on all sides onto the white fabric. For the backing of the goose, use the posterboard body again to cut another white body exactly the size of the posterboard. Follow the same procedure with the feet and bill on the orange fabric.

Using the same technique as for the balloons, glue the white fabric to the body, clipping the fabric as necessary to make it fit the curves. Pad and cover the feet and bill pieces in the same manner. Placing the posterboard extensions under the body, glue the feet and bill in place. Glue a white fabric backing to the body to cover raw edges.

Plan the wall placement of the hanging by laying the entire assemblage on the floor and arranging it to look its best in the space available. Glue velcro fasteners to the backs of the goose and balloons and glue their counterparts to the wall in the positions you have calculated from your floor arrangement. Use three fasteners on the goose, one on each balloon. When all the glue is dry, hang the assemblage and pull the balloon cords together. Tie them tightly and place them under the goose's bill.

Match this line to line A
on body to draw complete
pattern

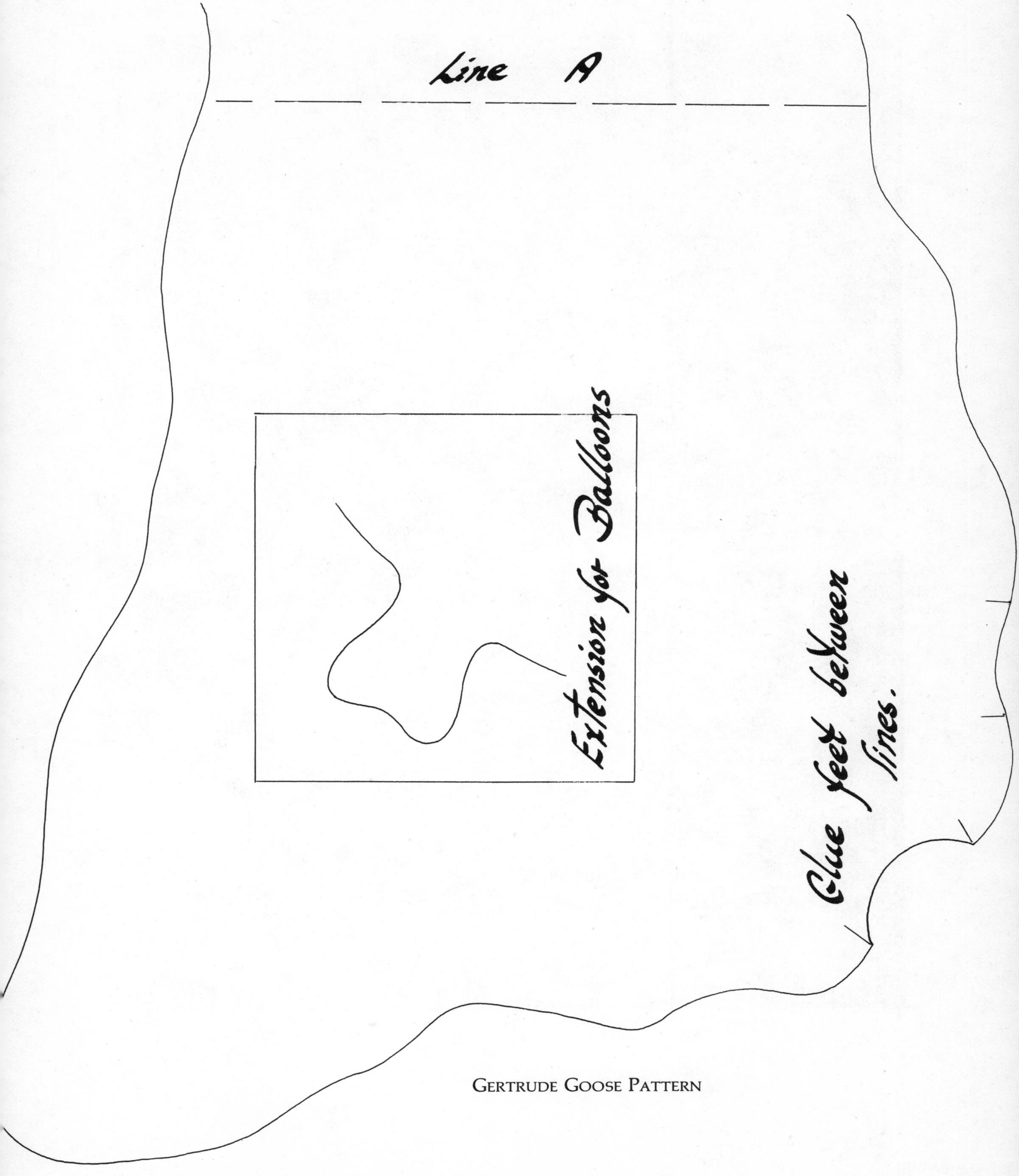

Line A

Extension for Balloons

Glue feet between lines.

GERTRUDE GOOSE PATTERN

Rainbow Comforter

Nothing could be more cheerful in the nursery than this gaily patterned, fluffy comforter. The goose and balloons carry out the theme and colors established by the soft Gertrude Goose Wall Hanging (page 70), and the bright rainbow adds another splash of vivid color. It would be fun to make a set of matching bumpers—plain yellow for the sides and foot of the crib, with an arch shaped and colored like a rainbow for the head of the bed.

This comforter is appliquéd by hand, but it could also be finished very quickly using a close zigzag stitch on the sewing machine, losing nothing in the design. Consider this alternative if time is at a premium.

SIZE
40 × 60 inches

MATERIALS
Broadcloth, 45 inches wide, yellow, 3½ yards
Broadcloth, 45 inches wide, pale blue, 1¾ yards
Broadcloth, 45 inches wide, ½ yard each of the following colors: red, orange, blue, dark green, purple, white

Broadcloth, 4 inch square, light green
Bias tape, extra-wide style (1-inch), dark blue, 2 packages
Interfacing, fusible type, light weight, 2 yards
Quilt filler, crib size, extra fluffy type
Embroidery floss, 1 skein each of the following colors: orange, blue, light blue, dark green, light green, purple, white. Also, 2 skeins each red and yellow. (Match the broadcloth colors.)
Sewing thread, orange, blue, light blue, dark green, light green, red, purple and white

INSTRUCTIONS
Cut two pieces of yellow fabric 41 inches wide and 61 inches long. From the pale blue fabric, cut two pieces 7 × 61 inches and two pieces 7 × 41 inches. Placing the blue over the yellow and mitering the corners, baste the blue to the yellow to form a frame for the comforter top. Baste both edges of the frame to the yellow.

Draw a grid of 1-inch squares on a large sheet of paper and use the grid to enlarge the accompanying diagram of the rainbow and

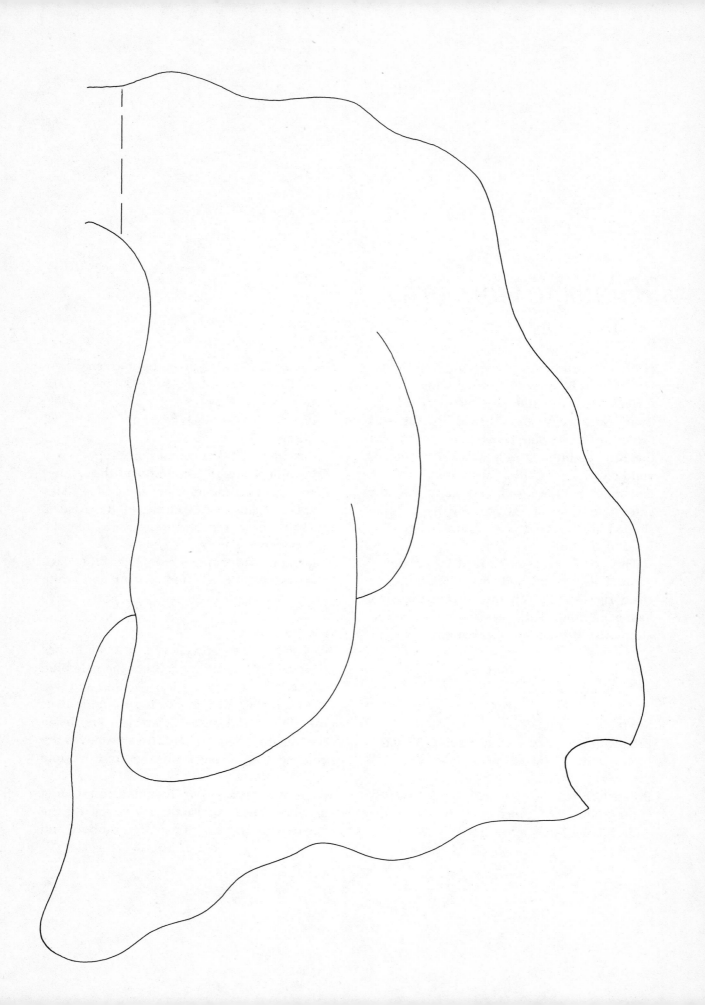

PATTERN FOR GOOSE FOR RAINBOW
COMFORTER

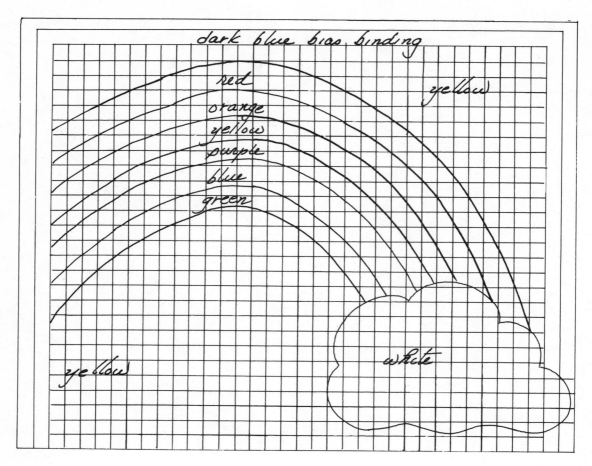

PATTERN FOR RAINBOW

cloud, matching square for square. Cut the enlarged drawing into two pattern pieces, the rainbow and the cloud. Using the pattern pieces as a guide, cut a rainbow and cloud from the fusible interfacing.

Next cut apart the rainbow pattern on the curved lines dividing the colors and use the individual pieces as guides for cutting the various colors of fabric. Following the drawing as a guide for color placement, lay the fabric pieces on the fusible interfacing rainbow, placing them as close together as possible. Fuse to the interfacing.

Machine-stitch around each color of the rainbow, staying as close as possible to the raw edges. Matching the thread color to one of the fabric colors—use green between the green and blue, blue between the blue and purple, purple next followed by yellow and orange—and using two strands of embroidery floss and the Herringbone Stitch, work a wide row of stitches to cover the machine stitching and the raw edges.

Fuse the fabric cloud to the interfacing. Place the rainbow and cloud on the background as shown in the diagram. Baste in place, leaving the cloud unfastened where it overlaps the pale blue frame. Machine stitch. Baste the dark blue bias tape around the inner edge of the pale blue frame, covering the raw edges of the frame and the rainbow on the left side and slipping it under the cloud on the right. Machine stitch both sides of the tape down.

Using matching embroidery floss, Blanket Stitch over the machine stitching around the outline of the rainbow and cloud.

Cut nine balloons from the colored fabric using a glass or cup with a 3½-inch diameter as a guide. Make a small extension that looks like the knotted end of a balloon using the drawing for the Gertrude Goose Wall Hanging (page 73) as a model. Make two light blue balloons and one each in red, orange, yellow, purple, light green, and dark green. Fuse each to the interfacing and machine-stitch around the outside edges. Arrange at random with some partially overlapping and some on the cloud. Baste in place and then Blanket Stitch around each with matching embroidery floss.

Trace the goose and cut the form from both the interfacing and the white fabric. Trace the feet and bill and cut them from the interfacing and the orange fabric. Bond the fabric pieces to the interfacing. Baste to the coverlet in the left lower corner as pictured, with the left foot about 1½ inches from the blue border and the tail about 1 inch inside the border. Machine-stitch. Embroider the wing line with pale blue floss and Outline Stitch. Outline the eye with pale blue and work the pupil with darker blue in Satin Stitch. Blanket Stitch around the entire goose with matching embroidery thread.

Lightly mark the lines for the balloon strings and embroider them with red Chain Stitch.

Feather Stitch along the inside edge of the dark blue binding with two strands of green. Place a red French Knot at the end of each arm of the stitches. Repeat on the outside edge, using yellow for the Feather Stitch and orange for the French Knots.

Press well. With the right sides together, stitch the comforter top to the yellow backing, leaving the bottom open for turning. Lay the quilt filler on top of the unturned unit. Baste it to the seam allowance with long, loose stitches. Turn. Close the opening with invisible stitches.

Making very light markings, divide the yellow field into 5-inch squares, making a mark only at the corners of each square. Using six strands of yellow embroidery floss, tuft the comforter at each mark. Do not tuft in the areas of the design, however—the goose, rainbow, etc. Work only as many tufts as fall into the plain yellow fabric.

To tuft: Thread the needle with a long strand of floss. Bring the needle up from the back, leaving a 2-inch tail. Make a small stitch and return the needle to the back. Tie the thread into a square knot and run the threaded needle into the quilt body. Cut the end off short and it will disappear. Thread the loose end into a needle and pull it into the quilt body again, cutting it off short.

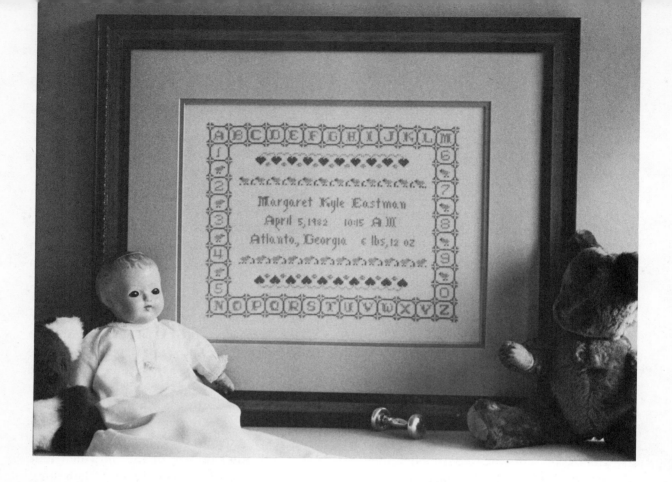

ABC Birth Record

Why not begin your own new tradition by making each new baby as it comes along an embroidered birth record? This one, patterned after an old schoolgirl's sampler, is updated with bright colors and looks like a lot more work than is actually involved.

This Cross Stitch sampler was worked on Davosa even-weave fabric with twenty-eight threads to the inch, but each cross was made over two threads so the stitches are actually fourteen to the inch—small enough to be pretty, but not so time-consuming as very tiny stitches can be. The design can also be worked on canvas, even-weave linen, or Aida or Hardanger fabrics.

SIZE
10 × 13 inches (design area only)

MATERIALS
Davosa fabric, cream, 28 count, 18 × 21 inches
Embroidery floss, DMC, 1 skein each as follows: 813, blue; 352, light coral; 351, coral; 369, light green; 744, yellow; 741, orange. Also, two skeins 368, green.

INSTRUCTIONS
Cut the fabric on a thread to make certain it is straight. Hem or zigzag around the edges to prevent fraying. Run a colored basting

horizontally and vertically to mark the center of the piece.

Begin working wherever it pleases you. I like to start at the top center of the border, measuring down 4 inches from the top and starting with the green lattice. I keep three needles threaded and work the flowers and lattice as I go, working first to the right edge and then returning to the center to work to the left.

Note that portions of the design overlap on the charts. This is to help you move from one page to another.

Work all stitches with two strands of floss.

Make each Cross Stitch over a square of two threads and remember to figure this in when counting threads between motifs. For a smoother, more professional look, always cross all stitches in the same direction.

Complete the border and the two rows of chicks and hearts. Count and mark the positions of the rows of print.

Lay out the baby's name, date, place of birth or birth weight, etc., on graph paper using the capital letters found in the border of the diagram and lowercase letters and numerals from the accompanying chart, spacing the letters as they are on the chart and sampler. Count to find the center of each line and begin embroidering from that point.

Block and frame as shown.

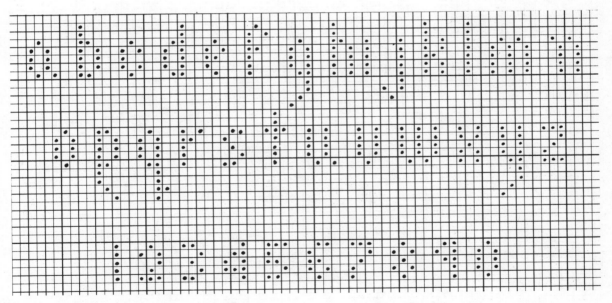

NUMERALS AND LOWERCASE ALPHABET

center

center

COLORS

- 813 blue
- 352 light coral
- 351 coral

✖ 369 light green
· 368 green
╱ yellow
✖ orange

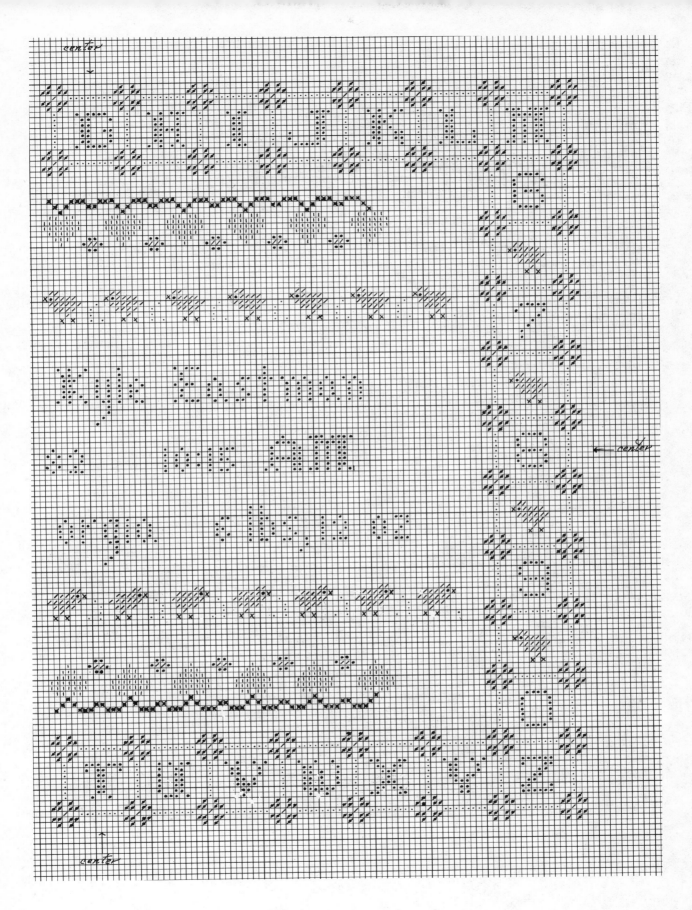

Ribbons-and-Toys Birth Record

Baby's favorite toys are here on this little picture to record his birthday. There's a cuddly teddy bear, a woolly lamb, a big-eared bunny sitting on a ruffled pillow, a soft yellow duck, a silly roly-poly, and some packages still to be opened. Ribbon bows abound—a big one encloses the written data and small ones are on the packages, pillow, and the animals. This record is a sweet remembrance to hang in the nursery, and a thoughtful gift.

SIZE
6¼ × 7½ inches (embroidered area only)

MATERIALS
Linen, pale ecru, 13 × 14½ inches

Embroidery floss, DMC, 1 skein each as follows: 963, pale pink; 894, medium pink; 827, pale blue; 813, medium blue; 369, pale green; 368, medium green; 746, cream; 3078, yellow; 741, orange; 950, beige; white. Also one needleful of black.

Framing materials as shown are: 11 × 14-inch frame, precut pale blue mat with an 8 × 10-inch oval opening; 11 × 14-inch piece of polyester quilt filler

INSTRUCTIONS
Trace the design and the lines for the birth record information. Using your own script or the alphabet on page 86, fill in the baby's first name on the top line, the date of birth on the next line, time of birth on the third line, and the birth weight on the last line. Space the letters as shown on the alphabet chart and center the information on each line.

Turn the paper over and go over all the lines—except the base lines for the lettering—with a transfer pencil. With a hot iron, transfer the design to the linen.

Work the design using the colors and stitches indicated in the diagram. Use two strands of embroidery floss except where otherwise indicated.

BOW

Work the large bow in pale blue Satin Stitch, then outline it with Back Stitch with a single strand of medium pink, placing the stitches as close as possible to the edge of the ribbon.

BUNNY

Work the body in random Long and Short Stitch to create a textured look; change directions slightly to fit curves and give the illusion of roundness. Fill in the tail with French Knots placed as close together as possible. Work the jacket, nose, and ear details with pale pink in Satin Stitch. To suggest a shadow, make a long stitch with pale blue at the right side of the pink detail on the full ear. Use pale blue Satin Stitch for the eyes and suggest a pupil with a small black Straight Stitch. Use three small Straight Stitches and a single strand of pale blue to make the seam stitches in the face. Outline all outside edges and all details with a single strand of medium blue, working as close as possible to the other embroidery so this blue outline is like a shadow effect.

Work the bow and pillow in Satin Stitch. Use the shades of blue as indicated for the

COLORS

963	pale pink
894	medium pink
827	pale blue
813	medium blue
369	pale green
368	medium green
746	cream
3078	yellow
741	orange
950	beige
	white
	black

STITCHES

a	Satin
b	Back
c	Outline
d	French Knot
e	Straight
f	Long and Short

bow and change directions with the Satin Stitch to separate the parts of the bow. Add a little bit of shading to the bow by making Straight Stitches with one strand of medium blue in the fold lines of the bow and by outlining the knot itself with the darker blue. Outline the eyelet ruffle and make tiny dots to indicate embroidery on it with a single strand of the medium blue and Back Stitch.

ALPHABET FOR RIBBONS-AND-TOYS BIRTH RECORD

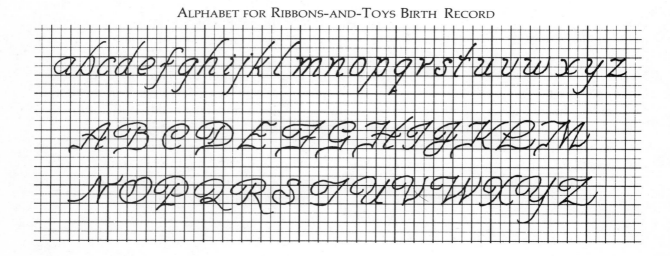

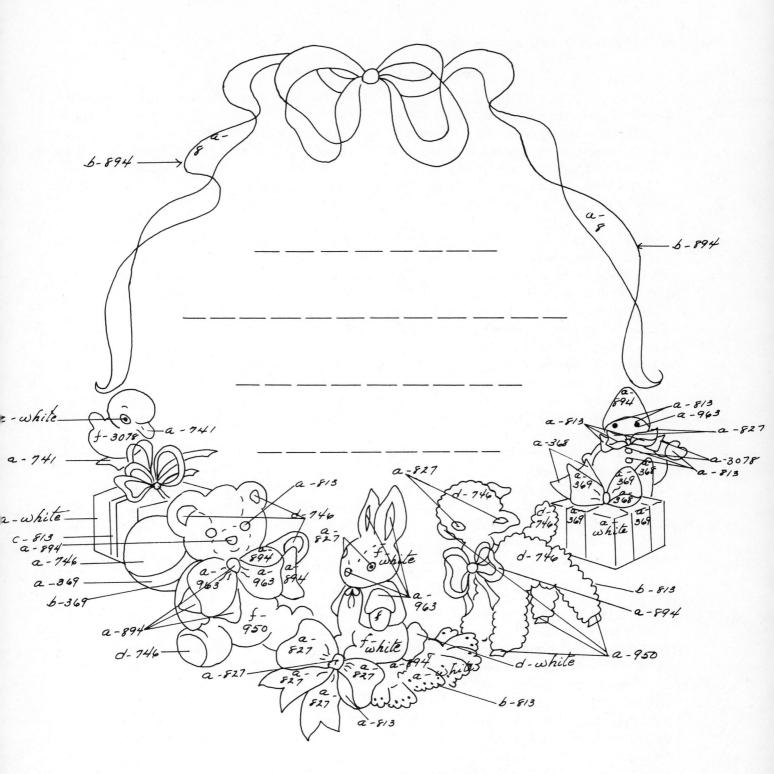

MOTIF FOR RIBBONS-AND-TOYS BIRTH RECORD

LAMB

Work the eye, hooves, nose, and bow in Satin Stitch in the colors noted on the chart. Use the single strand of black to make a small Straight Stitch to indicate the pupil in the eye. Outline the entire body with a single strand of medium blue and Back Stitch.

BOX BESIDE LAMB

Work the box, bow, and ribbons in Satin Stitch, laying the stitches vertically on the front and sides of the box. Slant the stitches to create perspective on the top of the box. Outline the box with a single strand of pale blue and Back Stitch. Use a single long stitch and the pale blue to mark the corners and fold lines of the box.

Work the ribbon and bow in Satin Stitch and give them definition by slanting the stitches differently in the various sections. Also add some shadows to the bow itself by making some straight stitches with the darker green to show the fold lines.

ROLY-POLY

Work entirely in Satin Stitch in the colors shown on the chart.

TEDDY BEAR

Using beige floss and random Long and Short Stitches, work the body. Change directions in the stitching to suggest roundness and to separate parts of the body. Use French Knots and cream thread for the pads on the paw and foot and the ear details. Use medium blue Satin Stitch for the eyes and then make a small white stitch on each for a pupil. With medium pink, make a Straight Stitch for the mouth; use the same pink and Satin Stitch for the nose. Work the ribbon bow in Satin Stitch, placing the two shades of pink as noted. Add some shading by outlining the knot with the darker pink and make a few straight stitches to add shading to the bow itself.

BALL

Work in Satin Stitch using the pale green and cream colors noted. Outline with a single strand of pale green and Back Stitch.

BOX

Work the bow and ribbons using medium blue floss and closely spaced rows of Outline Stitch. Use Satin Stitch to work the box to correspond to the first one. Use pale blue for outlines and details, as in the other box.

DUCK

Work the body in random Long and Short Stitches, changing directions to indicate roundness. Make the bill and foot in orange Satin Stitch. Use white Satin Stitch for the eye and use the black to indicate the pupil. Make a tiny Straight Stitch for the eyebrow.

LETTERING

Work the lettering in small Back Stitch using the medium green floss. Then take a single strand of the pale green and whip the Back Stitch to add continuity to the stitches.

FINISHING

Block and frame as shown, using the oval mat and putting the quilt filler behind the linen to give it a slightly padded appearance.

Baby Suzy

Rag dolls have appealed to countless generations of children. Toy museums and antique doll shows display a rich variety of other types of dolls, many resplendent in silks and lace and looking almost as new as the day they were bought, but a rag doll in original condition is a rarity. Rag dolls are so well loved and played with that few survive.

A friend of mine owns the remnants of an eighteenth-century cloth doll. She has no face or hair, the fabric has grayed to a dull patina, and stuffing is protruding from places

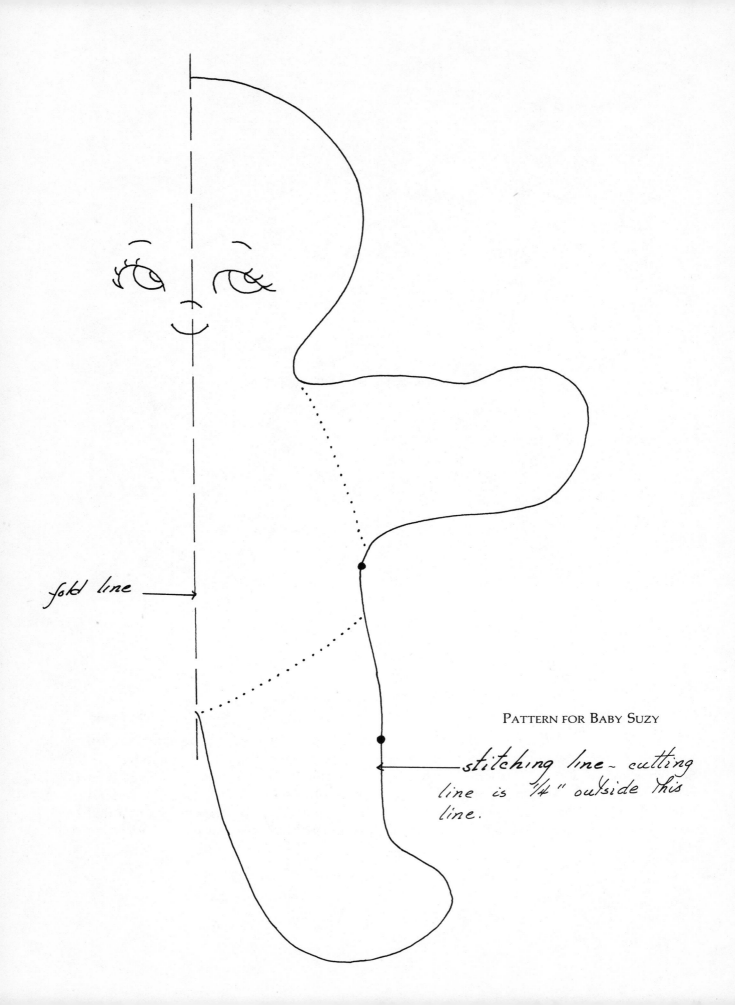

fold line

PATTERN FOR BABY SUZY

stitching line – cutting line is ¼" outside this line.

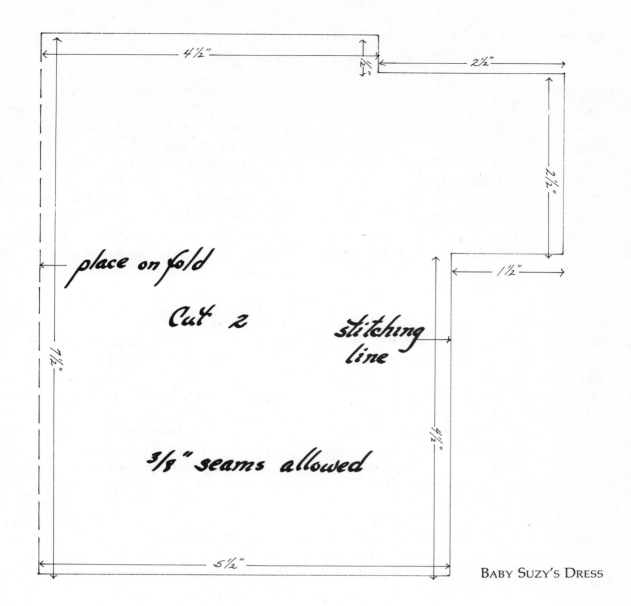

place on fold

Cut 2

3/8" seams allowed

stitching line

4½"

½"

2½"

2½"

1½"

7½"

5½"

4½"

BABY SUZY'S DRESS

where the fabric has rotted, but she is enthroned in the place of honor in an antique high chair and could not be purchased for any amount of money.

Your Baby Suzy may never achieve such exalted status, but you will enjoy making her and the little one who receives her will love her. She is a cuddly 8½-inch charmer. Her body is made in two pieces, her face is em-broidered with easy stitches, and her hair is yellow yarn French Knots. Her lace-trimmed dress is cut from two pieces, and elastic gathers the neck and sleeves. You can add a petticoat and diaper if you wish.

SIZE
8½ inches tall

MATERIALS

Pink cotton fabric, 11 × 18 inches

Printed fabric for dress, 8 × 14 inches

Narrow cotton lace, 1¾ yards

Elastic, ⅛ inch wide, 6 inches

Ribbon, ⅛ inch wide, ½ yard

Polyester fiberfill, small amount for stuffing

Sport weight yarn for hair, yellow, ¼ ounce

Small amounts of cotton embroidery floss for face: pink, red, blue, white, and brown

Sewing thread, pink for doll; white or matching color for dress

INSTRUCTIONS

Fold a piece of tracing paper in half lengthwise. Open it flat and match the fold to the dashed line on the drawing for the body. Trace. Fold the paper again on the fold line and trace through the paper to make the complete doll pattern. Go over the outline with an embroidery transfer pencil and transfer the pattern with a hot iron to the pink fabric, making two copies. Transfer the face to one copy only.

Embroider the face. Use small Split Stitches for all outlines, Satin Stitch for the eyes. Make the mouth red; nose pink; eyebrows, lashes, and outline of eyes brown; pupils blue with a white accent.

Cut out the two body pieces on a line ¼ inch *outside* the stitching line. With right sides together, stitch the two together, leaving an opening between dots on one side only. Trim the seam and clip the curves. Turn. Stuff the hands and feet first, working small amounts of filler at a time into them. Stuff the balance of the body and close the opening with invisible stitches. Quilt through all layers on the dotted lines to form "joints."

DRESS

Cut the two dress pieces according to the measurements on the diagram. Make all the seams ⅜ inch wide. Sew the shoulder seams. Press open. Make a narrow hem at the sleeve edge. Sew lace to the edge. Cut a piece of elastic 1¾ inches long and sew it to the sleeve ¼ inch from the edge, pulling the elastic tightly to make the edge ruffle.

Press the neck extensions to the inside and sew to form a casing on each side. Sew lace to the top edge. Insert a piece of elastic on each side, fastening each well at both ends.

Sew the sleeve and side seams. Press open.

Finish the bottom with a narrow hem edged with lace. Tie the ribbon in a bow and tack it to the front neck edge.

Baby Print Teddy Bears

Make one Teddy Bear or a basketful—Baby will love either! Look for a variety of tiny flowered prints or small-scaled ginghams to make these easy little toys. They are huggable and chewable and so often turn out to be that one special cherished toy that goes wherever Baby goes.

SIZE
6½ inches tall

MATERIALS
For one bear:
Print fabric, about 8 × 14 inches
Small amounts of embroidery floss for face.

93

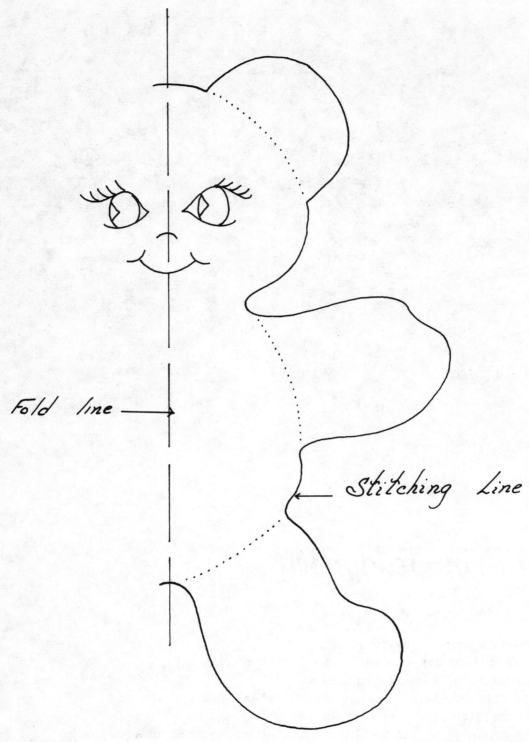

Fold line →

Stitching Line ←

PATTERN FOR TEDDY BEAR

Choose colors that will contrast with the print colors. Some of the bears shown have brown eyes outlined in black; one has blue eyes with brown outlines and lashes. Use pink or black for nose, red for the mouth.

Polyester fiberfill, small amount

Ribbon, ¼ inch wide, ½ yard

Sewing thread to match fabrics

INSTRUCTIONS

Fold a piece of tracing paper in half. Open flat and trace the stitching line and the face, matching the fold line of the paper to the dashed line on the drawing. Fold the paper again and trace the outline through the paper to form a complete bear. Go over the outlines with an embroidery transfer pencil and transfer the design with a hot iron to the fabric. You need transfer only the outline for the front of the bear.

Leave the fabric uncut. Embroider the face. Use Satin Stitch for the eyes and work all other lines in Outline Stitch.

With a long sewing machine stitch, run a row of stitching on the stitching line around the entire outline of the bear. (This will be a guide for stitching in the next step.)

Fold the fabric in half with the right sides together and carefully stitch the outline of the bear, following the line of sewing machine stitching. Leave about 1½ inches open for turning and stuffing. Trim away excess fabric, leaving a narrow seam allowance. Trim close to the stitching line at the inner arms and between the legs. Turn. Stuff. Close the opening with invisible stitches. Quilt through all layers on the dotted lines to form "joints" and to define the ears. Add a jaunty bow.

Teddy Bear Crib Garland

Four bright little teddy bears strung on a gay yellow ribbon will entertain a baby in the crib. These are made of felt, Blanket Stitched together, and stuffed lightly. Face and other accents are embroidered with cotton embroidery floss.

Not chewable so not good as toys, these little bears could however be used as package decorations or hung from a round mobile. They also make attractive Christmas tree decorations!

SIZE
Each bear, 4½ inches high

MATERIALS
Felt, assorted colors, 5 × 9 inches for each bear
Embroidery floss, colors to compliment felt, small amounts of each color
Polyester fiberfill, a handful for each bear
Beads, wood or plastic, 5
Ribbon, ½ inch wide, 2 yards

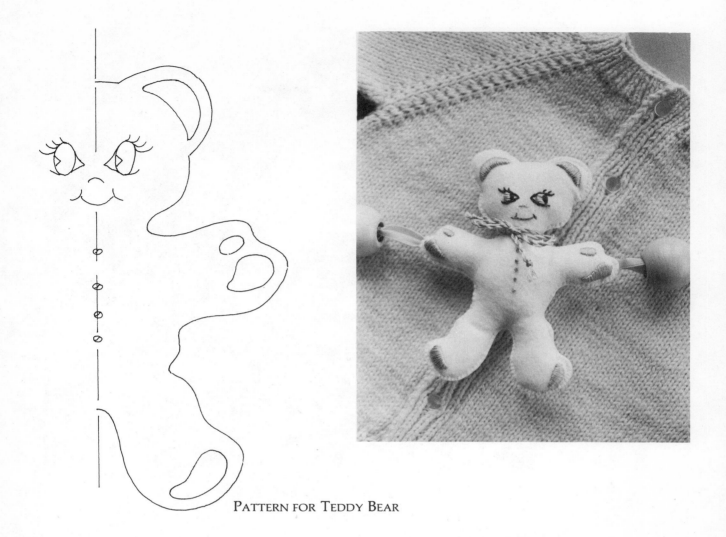

PATTERN FOR TEDDY BEAR

INSTRUCTIONS

On tracing paper make a transfer pattern as for Baby Suzy (page 90) and stamp it twice on each piece of felt, omitting the face on one transfer.

Using two strands of brightly colored embroidery floss and Satin Stitch, embroider the details of ears, paws, feet, and eyes. Make French Knot buttons; finish the other features with Outline Stitch.

Cut out the two pieces of bear on the solid line. Place together with the right sides out. With a single strand of embroidery floss of a color matched to the felt, fasten the two sides together with small Buttonhole Stitches. Leave an opening for the stuffing.

Stuff lightly, working small amounts of filler at a time into the body. Use the eraser end of a pencil to work the stuffing into the paws and feet if necessary. Close the opening with invisible stitches.

Make a twisted Bishop Cord Tie for a bow at the neck or use narrow ribbon to make a jaunty tie. Tack the bears to the ribbon, alternating them with the beads as shown in the photograph. Tie to the crib side.

97

Baby Elephant Chain

Baby will be delighted with this quartet of bright stuffed elephant babies suspended on the crib rail. Make the four, each in a different vivid pastel color, each with a different all-over embroidery pattern, with the chain to hang on the crib for a very young baby. Take it apart later to make four cute little stuffed animals just the size for tiny hands.

The embroidery adds interest to the over-all effect of these toys, making them appear to have been cut from printed fabrics; it also adds texture which the baby will begin to enjoy when playing with the elephants. This is an unusual gift, but one that does not require a lot of time to make.

SIZE

Each elephant, 8 inches from tip of trunk to back foot

MATERIALS

Broadcloth, 45 inches wide, blue, yellow, pink, and green, ¼ yard each (or scraps sufficient to cut two body pieces and four ear pieces of each color)

Embroidery floss, less than 1 skein each of pink, light red, cream, yellow, bright yellow, medium blue, and medium green

Polyester fiberfill, a few handfuls for each elephant

Ribbon, yellow, ½ inch wide, 3 yards

Sewing thread to match fabric colors

INSTRUCTIONS

Trace the body of the elephant, including all the features to be embroidered, the stitching line for the ear, and the small dots scattered over the piece. (These dots are guides for placement of the embroidery patterns which are worked freehand over them.)

Using a transfer pencil and hot iron (see page 133), transfer the body pattern once on each color fabric. Turn the design transfer paper itself over and trace the design again with the transfer pencil to reverse the pattern. Transfer this side onto another piece of each color fabric.

It will be necessary to make four ear pieces for each elephant. Trace the pattern as you did for the body. Transfer the dots on only two of each color, as only the exposed sides of the ears need be embroidered.

Do not cut out either bodies or ear pieces until after the embroidery has been completed.

Using four strands of floss, embroider the elephants as follows: Work features and line details in Outline Stitch; use Buttonhole for "toes." Use a few Satin Stitches to fill in the eyes.

BLUE ELEPHANT

Use yellow thread for the features, toes, and outlines. Also with yellow, embroider a Cross Stitch plus a long vertical stitch over each dot. Place a red stitch horizontally across the three to make a configuration like that shown in Embroidery Detail #1.

GREEN ELEPHANT

Use pink thread for the features, toes, and outlines. Following Embroidery Detail #2 and using pink, make a Lazy Daisy Stitch on each dot, placing the stitch so the base is on the dot. Place a yellow Fly Stitch at the base of the Lazy Daisy Stitch, making the tie-down stitch just below it.

PINK ELEPHANT

Use green to embroider the features, toes, and outlines. Using bright yellow thread, make a French Knot on each dot. Following Embroidery Detail #3 and using the cream-colored floss, make a five-petaled Lazy Daisy Stitch flower around each French Knot.

YELLOW ELEPHANT

Embroider the features, toes, and outlines with blue floss. With bright yellow, make a French Knot over each dot. Following Embroidery Detail #4, make a small flower by placing five blue French Knots evenly spaced around the yellow center.

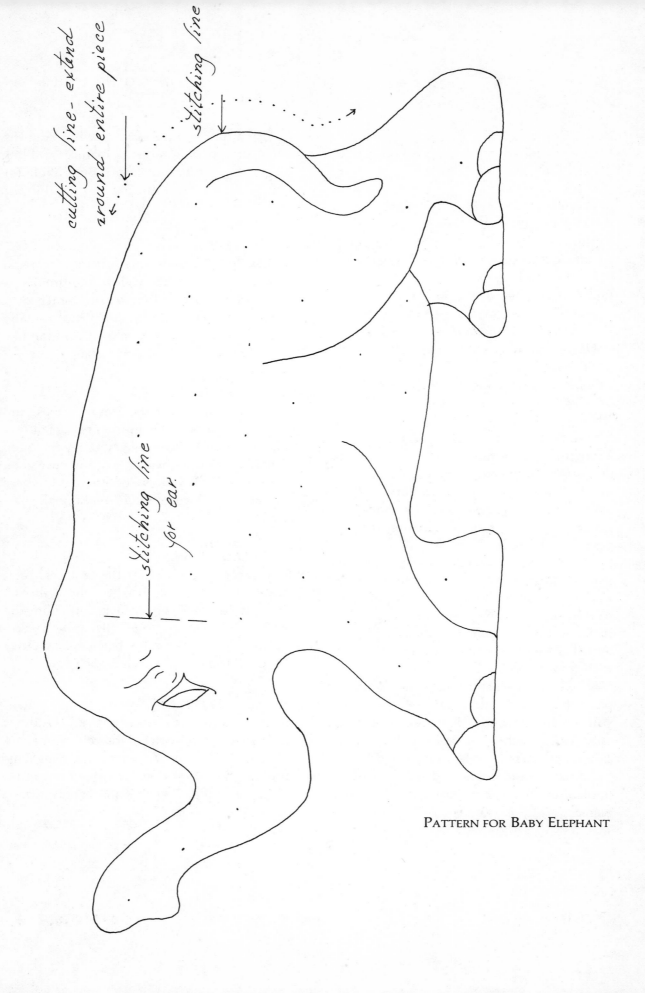

cutting line - extend around entire piece

stitching line

stitching line for ear

PATTERN FOR BABY ELEPHANT

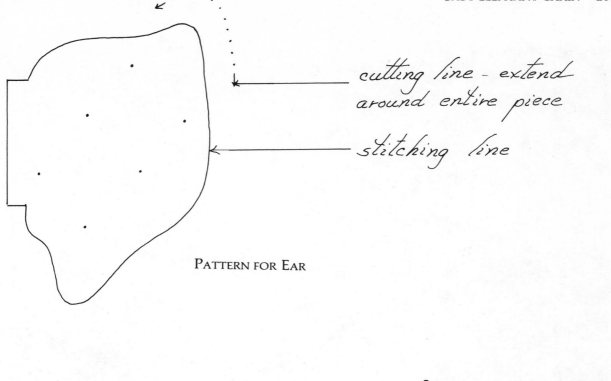

cutting line - extend around entire piece

stitching line

PATTERN FOR EAR

BABY ELEPHANT EMBROIDERY DETAILS

1

2

3

4

CONSTRUCTION

Press each embroidered piece well. Cut out the body pieces carefully on the *cutting line.* With the right sides together, sew the fronts to the backs, leaving them open between the legs for stuffing. Trim the seams at the corners and clip where necessary. Turn. Stuff until nicely plump but not hard. Close the opening.

As noted, only two ear pieces need be embroidered for each elephant. Work these to match the patterns on the bodies. Press.

With the right sides together, sew one embroidered ear piece to one plain one, leaving the straight side open for stuffing. Trim the seam and turn. Stuff lightly. Close the opening and sew the ear to the line on the head.

To make the elephant chain, tack the trunks to the tails as shown. Cut two 1½-yard lengths of ribbon. Fold each in half and, sewing through the fold, attach one to each end of the chain. Tie the ribbon in bows on the crib side rail.

Bassinet

An old-fashioned wicker bassinet is sweet without any trimming, but when fitted with a white quilted liner and ruffled batiste skirt it becomes a very special piece of nursery furniture.

Although the bassinet pictured is thirty-five years old, practically identical models are available new. Nothing about them seems to have changed. This one has had numerous petticoats made for it—some dotted swiss, one with eyelet embroidery, most of batiste or lawn—but all had the same basic design feeling. They add luxury to a purely practical little bed and make it fun to use.

Choose batiste or lawn that is predominantly polyester—65 percent polyester, 35 percent cotton is a good blend—so your skirt is easy to care for. The new quilted cottons make soft liners that add luxury yet are completely practical.

MATERIALS

Most bassinets are of the same general size and shape, but they vary just enough so that you will have to measure your own and change the quantities of materials specified to fit. The following materials and yardages, used for the skirt pictured, should be considered as approximations only.

Quilted fabric, white, 45 inches wide,
  1 yard
Batiste, white, 45 inches wide, 8 yards
Muslin, white, 45 inches wide, 4 yards
Bias binding, white, 1 package
Lace, 2 inches wide, 5 yards
Lace, 1 inch wide, 10 yards
Ribbon, 1½ inches wide, pale blue,
  5 yards
Sewing thread, white
Elastic, 1¼ inches wide, 2¼ yards
Velcro fasteners, ⅜ inch size, 15

INSTRUCTIONS

LINER

Cut a piece of muslin to fit the bottom of the bassinet, adding a ½ inch seam allowance all around.

Measure the height of the side walls and cut the quilted fabric to fit, adding a ½ inch seam allowance all around. Note that the walls slope outward slightly. For a smooth fit it will probably be best to cut the liner in four pieces—two long ones for the sides and two smaller ones for the ends. Cut the pieces slightly wider at the top (with the side edges slanting outwards at equal angles) to accommodate the slope of the walls. Seam the pieces together and stitch them to the muslin cut to fit the bottom of the bassinet.

Cut a 5-inch-wide piece of quilted fabric to fit over the rim of the bassinet. Sew this to the top of the liner to form a cuff which folds down over the outside. Bind the edges of the cuff with bias tape.

SKIRT

The bassinet pictured is 27 inches from the top edge to the floor and measures 90 inches around the top circumference. Four widths of 45-inch batiste were used for the skirt, eight widths for the ruffle, and the finished length including the ruffle is 26½ inches.

The skirt was cut as follows: Ruffle, eight widths 16 inches deep; skirt, four widths, 30 inches long. All tucks are ¾-inch, requiring 1½ inches of extra fabric each to be added to the required finished length of the pieces.

Seam the eight lengths of ruffle together at the 16-inch edges to form a continuous piece. Press the seams open. Turn up and stitch a double 2-inch hem. Measure up from the top of the hem 2¼ inches and press a fold line for the first tuck. Fold the fabric on the line and stitch the tuck ¾ inch from the fold. Press the tuck toward the hem. Measure up 2½ inches from the stitching of the tuck and mark the fold line for the next tuck. Stitch and press the tuck in the same manner. Repeat for one more tuck. Sew the 1-inch-wide lace over the stitching of the hem. The finished ruffle measures 7½ inches.

Seam the four widths of the skirt together at the 30-inch edges to make a continuous piece. Measure up from the lower edge 6 inches and press a line for the first tuck. Stitch a ¾-inch tuck on the line. Press the tuck toward the bottom of the piece. Measure up 1½ inches from the stitching line and place another tuck. Make a third tuck spaced evenly above the other two. Press all tucks toward the bottom of the piece.

Measure up from the stitching line of the last tuck 1 inch and sew the 2-inch lace on that line. Stitch both edges of the lace to the skirt.

Measure up 2½ inches from the top of the lace and press a line for a tuck. Stitch a ¾-inch tuck and make two more above it, each spaced 1½ inches above the last. Press all tucks to the bottom of the skirt.

Gather the top of the ruffle to fit the bottom of the skirt, pin it distributing the gathers evenly, and sew.

Cut four widths of lining the same length as the finished skirt plus 1 inch. Sew the seams; press the seams open. Turn up and stitch a 2-inch hem.

With the right sides together, stitch the lining to the skirt along the top edge. Turn. Press. Stitch around the top ¼ inch from the fold, then again 1½ inches from the first stitching line to form a casing. Cut a piece of elastic to fit snugly around the top of the bassinet. With a seam ripper, open one of the lining seams inside the casing stitching to allow the insertion of the elastic. Insert the elastic.

Fit the skirt onto the bassinet and adjust the gathers. Mark positions for the Velcro fasteners on both the skirt and the padded lining cuff, placing them about 6 inches apart. Sew on the fasteners.

Make a large bow as shown and attach it to the skirt with a few easy-to-remove stitches so it can come off easily when the skirt is laundered.

Infant Seat Pad Cover

The infant seat, a simple plastic basket with many names, is undoubtedly the most useful piece of nursery equipment ever invented. Most come equipped with a pad and safety belt, but the plastic cover on the pads leaves much to be desired. Many kinds of fabric-covered pads are available, but this is definitely something you can make better yourself and for far less money. Your pad will be one of a kind and will probably fit better since it will be made specifically for your seat instead of being a general size made to fit as many different brands of carriers as possible.

In anticipation of a little boy, this pad is made with crisp quilted gingham and finished with a white corded piping, giving it a tailored look. If you want to be fancier, you can use a flower print quilt and add an eyelet ruffle instead of piping. Quilted fabrics are now made in so many different prints and solids that your options are almost unlimited.

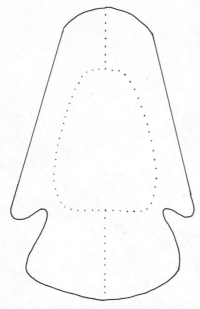

PATTERN FOR PAD COVER

MATERIALS

Quilted fabric, 45 inches wide, approximately 1 yard

Bias binding, 1 package

Cording, either purchased in a package or made from a piece of cord covered with a bias strip. Quantity needed: enough to reach around the entire outside edge of the pad

Snaps, size 1, 2

Sewing thread to match fabric

INSTRUCTIONS

Measure your pad before purchasing fabric to make certain that 1 yard is sufficient. Lay the pad flat and measure it at its widest point. Add 2 inches to this measurement. You will need to double this. (A pad that is 16 inches at its widest point will require 36 inches of fabric.)

The sketch shows the approximate shape of the pad for one popular carrier. Pads vary, so use your own for a pattern. The dotted lines on the sketch show the facings which form the back of the cover.

Lay your pad on the fabric—right side of the fabric up, right side of the pad up. With a soft pencil, draw an outline around the pad 1 inch from the pad edges all the way around. This extra inch allows for the seam and lets the cover give when it is fitted into the carrier.

Cut out the front cover on the pencil line. Lay the pad on the fabric and mark the openings for the safety straps. Make buttonholes the width of the straps at these marks.

Using the front as a pattern, cut two facing pieces similar to the ones shown by the dotted lines on the sketch. When cutting these pieces, allow a ½-inch extension on the two straight edges at the top and bottom of one piece.

Bind the two facing pieces along the dotted lines with the bias binding. With the right sides up, lay the facings in the position they will be in when the cover is finished. Overlap the straight edges ½ inch and pin. Top-stitch the two together for 2 inches at the very top and bottom.

Sew the cording to the right side of the entire outside edge of the cover front, clipping cording where necessary. With the right sides together, sew the front to the facings. Turn. Sew a snap to the openings of the top and bottom sections of the facing. Insert the pad and pull the safety straps through the buttonholes.

Knit Booties

New styles in baby footwear appear all the time and some are very cute and sturdy, but none has been able to replace the bootie for comfort and practicality. The new yarns make booties easy to care for and soft on Baby's feet. A pair—even with fancy lace cuffs—takes just about as little time as an evening's TV, so get your needles busy making Baby a bootie wardrobe!

SIZE
Infant

YELLOW QUAKER STITCH BOOTIES

MATERIALS
Baby yarn, yellow, 1 ounce
Knitting needles, size 2, 1 pair

YELLOW QUAKER STITCH BOOTIES

GAUGE
9 sts = 1 inch

INSTRUCTIONS
Cast on 44 sts.
Pattern (wrong side): *Row 1:*   K.
Row 2: P.
Row 3: K (one rib made).

Repeat these 3 rows for Quaker pattern nine times (five ribs on right side). Work 4 rows Stockinette St.

Beading Row: K 3, *K 2 tog, yo, K 2*, repeat between *'s across the row. P next row. K 1 row. P 1 row.

Instep: K across 28 sts. Turn. P across 12 sts. Work St St back and forth across these 12 sts of instep for 2 inches. End with K row.

Pick up and K 12 sts along side of instep. K the 16 sts on the left needle. K next row picking up 12 sts along the other side of the instep, K remaining 16 sts (68 sts). Continue working on the 68 sts in Gtr St for 8 rows.

Dec for foot: K 2 tog, K 30, K 2 tog twice, K 30, K 2 tog. K 1 row.
Dec Row: K 2 tog, K 28, K 2 tog twice, K 28, K 2 tog. K 1 row.

Continue decreasing every other row in the same manner, having 2 sts less between decreases each dec row, three times more (48 sts). K 1 row. Bind off. Sew seam. Block. Insert ribbon or Bishop Cord Ties in beading.

PINK SEED STITCH BOOTIES

MATERIALS
Baby yarn, pink, 1 skein
Knitting needles, size 2, 1 pair.

GAUGE
9 sts = 1 inch

INSTRUCTIONS
Cast on 48 sts. K 3 rows.

PINK SEED STITCH BOOTIES

Seed Stitch Pattern: Row 1: K 2, P 2 across
Row 2: K 2, P 2 across.
Row 3: P 2, K 2 across.
Row 4: P 2, K 2 across.

Repeat these 4 pattern rows for 2½ inches.
Beading Row: K 1, *K 2 tog, yo, K 2*, repeat across row. P 1 row.
Instep: K across 17 sts, change to Seed St pattern for next 14 sts of instep. Turn after 31 sts. Keeping the Seed St pattern, work back and forth on the 14 instep sts for 2 inches. End with the instep sts on the right needle.

Pick up and K 14 sts along side of instep, K across the 17 sts on left needle. K back to other side of instep, pick up and K 14 sts, finish row.

Work even in Gtr St for 8 rows.
Dec for foot: K 2 tog, K 34, K 2 tog twice, K 34, K 2 tog. K 1 row.
Dec row: K 2 tog, K 32, K 2 tog twice, K 32, K 2 tog. K 1 row.

Continue decreasing in this manner, having 2 sts less between decreases each dec row, two more times (60 sts). Bind off. Sew seam. Block. Insert Bishop Cord Ties or ribbon in beading.

PINK LACY-TOP BOOTIES

MATERIALS
Baby yarn, pink, 1 skein
Knitting needles, size 2, 1 pair

GAUGE
9 sts = 1 inch

PINK LACY-TOP BOOTIES

INSTRUCTIONS
Cast on 49 sts. K 3 rows.
Pattern: Row 1: *K 1, yo, K 1, sl 1, K 1, psso, K 5, K 2 tog, K 1, yo*, repeat between *'s ending yo, K 1.
Row 2: and all even rows—P.
Row 3: K 2, yo, *K 1, sl 1, K 1, psso, K 3, K 2 tog, K 1, yo, K 3, yo*, repeat across ending yo, K 2.
Row 5: K 3, *yo, K 1, sl 1, K 1, psso, K 1, K 2 tog, K 1, yo, K 5*, repeat across ending yo, K 3.
Row 7: K 4, *yo, K 1, sl 1, K 2 tog, psso, K 1, yo, K 7*, repeat across ending K 4.

Repeat the above pattern two times more. P 1 row.
Beading row: *K 2, K 2 tog, yo*, repeat across row. P 1 row.
Instep: Knit across 32 sts, turn, P across 15 sts. Work back and forth in St St on the center 15 sts for 2 inches. End with K row.

Pick up and K 12 sts along the side of the instep, continue to K across the 17 sts on the left needle. K across to other side of instep, pick up and K 12 sts, continue knitting to end of row (73 sts).

Work even in Gtr St for 8 rows.

Dec for foot: K 1, K 2 tog, K 31, K 2 tog, K 1, K 2 tog, K 31, K 2 tog, K 1. K 1 row.

Dec row: K 1, K 2 tog, K 29, K 2 tog, K 1, K 2 tog, K 29, K 2 tog, K 1. K 1 row.

Continue decreasing in this manner, having 2 sts less between decreases each dec row, two times more. Bind off. Sew seam. Block. Insert ribbon or Bishop Cord Ties in beading.

MARY JANES

MATERIALS

Baby yarn, white, 1 skein
Knitting needles, size 2, 1 pair
Buttons, white pearl, ¼ inch diameter, 2
Small amount of embroidery thread: pale blue, green, and yellow

MARY JANES

GAUGE

9 sts = 1 inch

INSTRUCTIONS

Cast on 48 sts.

Row 1: K 24, place a marker on needle, K 24.

Row 2: Inc 1 st in first st, K to last st before marker, inc 1 st, sl marker, inc 1 st in next st, K to last st, inc 1 st (52 sts).

Row 3: K, slipping marker.

Repeat Rows 2 and 3 two times (60 sts). K next row dropping marker.

Work even in Gtr St. for 16 rows.

Instep: Row 1: K 34, K 2 tog.

Row 2: Turn, sl 1, K 8, K 2 tog.

Repeat Row 2 eighteen times (40 sts). Turn, sl 1, K to end of row. Bind off.

Strap: Cast on 44 sts. K 1 row. Make buttonhole in next row as follows: K 2, yo, K 2 tog, K to end of row. K 1 row. Bind off.

EMBROIDERY

The Mary Janes pictured have three small rosebuds (Style 1, page 144) worked on the instep in pale blue with yellow French Knot centers and light green leaves. It is easier to do the embroidery before sewing the seams.

FINISHING

Sew the heel and sole seam. Sew the center of the strap to the back of the slipper, attaching a length of about ½ inch. Sew on button.

WHITE LACY-TOP BOOTIES

MATERIALS

Baby yarn, white, 1 skein
Knitting needles, size 2, 1 pair

WHITE LACY-TOP BOOTIES

GAUGE
9 sts = 1 inch

INSTRUCTIONS
Cast on 48 sts. K 3 rows.
Pattern: Row 1: K 2, *yo, K 2, sl 1, K 1, psso, K 2 tog, K 2, yo, K 1*, repeat between *'s ending K 2.
Row 2 and all even rows: P.
Row 3: K 1, *yo, K 2, sl 1, K 1, psso, K 2 tog, K 2, yo, K 1*, repeat between *'s across row ending K 3.
Row 4: P.

Repeat these 4 rows for pattern. Work even 2¼ inches, ending with P row.
Beading Row: *K 2, K 2 tog, yo*, repeat across row. P 1 row.
Instep: Knit across 32 sts, turn, P across 16 sts, work back and forth on the center 16 sts for 2 inches. End with K row.

Pick up and K 12 sts along side of instep, continue to K across the 16 sts on left needle.

Knit across to other side of instep, pick up and K 12 sts, continuing knitting to end of row (72 sts).

Work even in Gtr St for 8 rows.
Dec for foot: K 1, K 2 tog, K 31, K 2 tog twice, K 31, K 2 tog, K 1. K 1 row.
Dec row: K 1, K 2 tog, K 29, K 2 tog twice, K 29, K 2 tog, K 1. K 1 row.

Continue decreasing in this manner, having 2 sts less between decreases each dec row, two times more. Bind off. Sew seam. Block. Insert ribbon or Bishop Cord Ties in beading.

BLUE EMBROIDERED BOOTIES

MATERIALS
Baby yarn, blue, 1 skein
Fuzzy white yarn, acryllic, about 10 yards
Knitting needles, size 2, 1 pair

BLUE EMBROIDERED BOOTIES

GAUGE
9 sts = 1 inch

INSTRUCTIONS
Cast on 42 sts. Work 8 rows Gtr St. Change to St St for 6 rows. Return to Gtr St and work even until the piece measures 2¼ inches.

Beading row: *K 2, K 2 tog, yo*, repeat across the row. K 1 row.

Instep: K across 27 sts, turn, work back and forth on the last 12 sts in St St for 2¼ inches. End with a K row.

Pick up and K 13 sts along side of instep, K to end of row. K back to the other side of the instep, pick up and K 13 sts, finish row (68 sts).

Work even in Gtr St for 8 rows.

Dec for foot: K 1, K 2 tog, K 29, K 2 tog twice, K 29, K 2 tog, K 1. K 1 row.

Dec row: K 1, K 2 tog, K 27, K 2 tog twice, K 27, K 2 tog, K 1. K 1 row.

Continue decreasing in this manner, having 2 sts less between decreases each dec row, two times more. K 1 row. Bind off.

EMBROIDERY
For this embroidery choose a fuzzy synthetic yarn resembling mohair or angora.

Beginning at the point at which the instep joins the cuff, work a row of Blanket Stitches around the St St of the instep, placing the stitches about ⅛ inch apart and making them about 1 row deep.

At the center of the toe, make a little three-petal flower by making a French Knot and three Lazy Daisy stitches. Trim the St St band on the cuff with the same flowers, placing them as shown in the photograph.

FINISHING
Sew seam. Block. With the fuzzy yarn make Bishop Cord Ties and insert in beading.

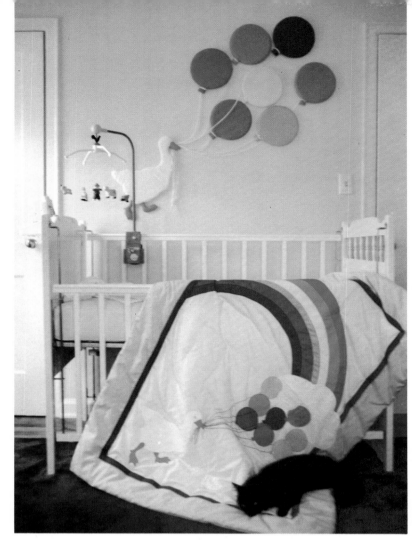

Gertrude Goose (*page 70*)
and Rainbow Comforter (*page 75*)

Shadow-Embroidered Comforter
(*page 60*) and Pillows (*page 68*)

Sunday Suits (*pages 26 and 35*), Heirloom Pillow (*page 14*)
and Baby Print Teddy Bears (*page 93*)

Heirloom Dress and Slip (*page 18*) and Smocked Bonnet (*page 24*)

Sweaters (*pages 116 and 118*), Booties (*page 107*) and Elephant Chain (*page 98*)

Kimono (*page 38*), Quilted Sacque and Bonnet (*page 42*) and Baby Suzy (*page 89*)

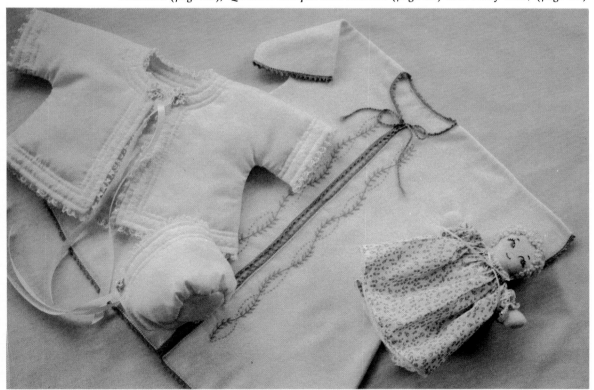

Bassinet (*page 102*), Infant Seat Pad Cover (*page 105*)
and ABC Birth Record (*page 80*)

Bibs (*page 56*), Flannel Sheets (*page 55*), Receiving Blankets (*page 51*)
and Teddy Bear Garland (*page 96*)

Rosebud Sacque and Booties

Imagine your favorite baby girl in this cuddly little knit set. She'll wear it on warm spring days with her prettiest dresses or as a dainty topping for her knit jump suits.

Knit of a sport-weight yarn, this set is a little heavier than those made of baby yarn, but still not bulky or heavy. The square neck and basic plain styling make it also appropriate for a little boy. The sacque can be made all in one color or the yoke and stripe around it can be of contrasting colors. It would be cute with a white yoke, blue stripe, and yellow body. Another combination would be to make the yoke and body of white with a stripe of yellow or blue.

SIZE
Six months. Chest 21 inches.

MATERIALS
Sport yarn, 50 gram balls, white, 2
Knitting needles, size 3, 1 pair
Steel crochet hook, size 7
Buttons, white, ¼ inch diameter, 4
Yarn for embroidery, approximately 10 yards each in medium pink, pale pink, and light green

GAUGE
7½ sts = 1 inch

SACQUE

INSTRUCTIONS
Body: Cast on 169 sts for lower edge. Work in St St (K 1 row, P 1 row) for 6 inches, ending with a P row.

Next row K 41, slip on holder for right front; bind off 8 sts for underarm; K 71, slip on holder for back; bind off 8 sts; finish row.
Left Front: Keeping the front edge even, dec 1 st at armhole edge every second row two times (39 sts). P 1 row, making a ridge on the right side. Continue in St St for 7 rows. P 1 row (ridge made). Work even in St St until 2¾ inches above underarm, ending at the front edge. Bind off 19 sts for neck; finish row. Work 6 rows even on 20 sts. Bind off for shoulder.
Back: Transfer the 71 sts of the back to needle. Beginning on the wrong side, continue to work St St, decreasing 1 st each side every second row two times. P next row to make a ridge. Work even in St St for 7 rows. P next

row making a ridge. Work even in St St until 3½ inches above underarm. Bind off.
Right Front: Take up the 41 sts of right front. Finish to match left front, binding off for neck at beg of K row.
Sleeves: Cast on 36 sts. Work in K 2, P 2 ribbing for 1½ inches. Inc 19 sts, spacing them evenly across the row (55 sts). Work even in St St for 5½ inches above the cuff, ending with a P row. Bind off 4 sts at beg of next 2 rows. Dec 1 st each side every second row two times (43 sts). P 1 row on right side to make a ridge. Work even in St St for 7 rows. P 1 row to make a ridge. Work 2 rows even. Dec 1 st each side next row. Bind off 3 sts at beg of next 4 rows. Bind off remaining 29 sts.

CONSTRUCTION
Sew shoulder and sleeve seams. Set in the sleeves, being careful to match ridges.

Working from the right side, crochet 2 rows single crochet around the neck, front, and lower edges, making four button loops on the second row on the right front edge of the yoke (left if for a boy). Sew on buttons. Block. Embroider according to instructions following booties.

BOOTIES

INSTRUCTIONS
Cast on 41 sts. K 7 rows. P 1 row, K 1 row - St St - for 6 rows. K 1 row (ridge made). Work in St St for 8 more rows.
Beading row: K 2, *K 2 tog, yo, K 3*, repeat to end of row ending K 3. Work in St St for 3 rows.
Instep: K 28, turn and work back and forth in

St St on the last 15 sts for 2 inches, ending with a K row. Pick up and K 12 sts along side of instep, K to end of row. Work back across the 40 sts, pick up and K 12 sts on the other side of the instep, and finish the row. Work even in Gtr St for 10 rows (65 sts). In last row dec 1 st.

Dec for foot: K 2 tog, K 28, K 2 tog twice, K 28, K 2 tog. K 1 row.

Dec row: K 2 tog, K 26, K 2 tog twice, K 26, K 2 tog. K 1 row.

Continue to decrease in this manner, always having 2 sts less between decreases each dec row, three times more. Bind off.

CONSTRUCTION

Embroider according to instructions that follow before sewing seams. Sew seams. Block. Insert ribbon or Bishop Cord Ties in beading.

EMBROIDERY

Since the sacque and booties are knit of an easy-care yarn, choose embroidery materials that will wash just as easily. Odds and ends of orlon baby yarn will be pretty. Cotton embroidery floss is also suitable. If finding the right shades in one or the other is difficult, use a combination of the two.

The rosebuds embroidered on the set in the photograph are Style 1 from page 144, but either of the other two styles will be pretty if you prefer them. The centers of the rosebuds are placed 1½ inches apart inside the pattern ridges around the yoke of the sacque and tops of the booties. One row is along the top edge of the ridge, the other is placed along the lower edge spaced evenly between the flowers of the row above.

SACQUE

To mark for even placement of the embroidery, measure in from the front edge of the sacque along the lower ridge 1 inch and make a small dot. Continue around the yoke, placing a dot every 1½ inches.

For the row along the top of the ridge, measure in from the front edge 1¾ inches and place the first dot. Continue around the yoke, placing the dots 1½ inches apart.

Rosebud Style 1 begins with a Satin Stitch center. Work the center of each rosebud with the deeper shade of pink and place it directly over the dot. Work the remainder of the rosebud with the pale pink and place a Lazy Daisy leaf on each side of the rosebud. Study the photograph as a reference for embroidering details.

BOOTIES

Embroider the cuffs, placing the rosebuds to match those on the sacque. Also work one rosebud on the toe of each bootie.

Raglan Cardigan

No sweater pattern is more elegant and comfortable than the classic raglan, and for very good reasons. The easy slope of the raglan shoulder always fits well and seems to grow with the child. The version described here may easily become the basic sweater for a baby's wardrobe since it is knit of easy-care orlon in colors that will mix with other clothing.

A feature of this sweater that makes it especially nice is that the front bands are ribbed and buttonholes are knit in. This avoids the necessity of binding the fronts with ribbon, which somehow always produces a lumpy look.

SIZE
Six months

MATERIALS
Baby yarn, 3 skeins
Knitting needles, 1 pair size 1, 1 pair size 3
Buttons, white pearl, ¼-inch diameter, 6

GAUGE
7½ sts = 1 inch on size 3 needles

NOTE
For a boy, make the buttonholes in the left front, as directed; place them in the right front for a girl.

INSTRUCTIONS
Beginning at the neck edge, cast on 93 sts on size 1 needles. Work in P 1, K 1 ribbing for 5 rows.
Buttonhole row: K 1, P 1, K 1, yo, K 2 tog, P 1, K 1 across the balance of row. (Repeat the buttonhole every 16th row.)

When 8 rows of ribbing have been completed, change to size 3 needles and begin raglan increases.
Raglan inc: Row 1 and all odd rows: P 1, K 1, over first 8 sts, P to last 8 sts, K 1, P 1 to end. Maintain this ribbed border to hem.
Row 2: K 1, P 1 over 8 sts, K 10 for left front, inc 1 st in next st, K 1, twist next 2 sts by knitting 2nd st on left needle before the first, inc 1 st in next st (seam pattern for raglan), K 6 for sleeve, inc 1 st in next st, K 1, twist next 2 sts, inc 1 st in next st (seam), K 25 for back, inc 1 st in next st, K 1, twist next 2 sts, inc 1 st in next st (seam), K 6 for sleeve, inc 1 st in next st, K 1, twist next 2 sts, inc 1 st in next st (seam), K 10 for right front, P 1, K 1 over remaining 8 sts.
Row 4: K 1, P 1 over 8 sts, K 11, inc 1 st in next st, K 1, twist next 2 sts, inc 1 st in next st, K 8, inc 1 st in next st, K 1, twist next 2 sts, inc 1 st in next st, K 27, inc 1 st in next st, K 1, twist next 2 sts, inc 1 st in next st, K 8, inc 1 st in next st, K 1, twist next 2 sts, inc 1 st in next st, K 11, P 1, K 1, over remaining 8 sts.

Continue to increase in this manner every other row until there are 19 increase rows and 245 sts.
Sleeves: Beginning on the right side, separate for the sleeve as follows: Knit the 40 sts of the left front and place on a holder. K next 49 sts of the left sleeve. Place the remaining sts on a holder.

Knit the 49 sts of the sleeve in St St, decreasing 1 st at each end of the second row and every 8th row twice thereafter (43 sts). Work even until the sleeve measures 5¾ inches from underarm. Change to size 1 needles and work in K 1, P 1 ribbing for 1½ inches. Bind off in ribbing.

Slip the sts from holder to needle. Attach yarn at the second raglan seam and K across the 67 sts of the back. Place these sts on a holder. K the 49 sts of the right sleeve. Slip the last 40 sts for right front to a holder.

Finish the right sleeve to correspond to the left.
Body: Slip the sts of the right front from holder to needle. Join yarn at underarm and K across ending with ribbed border. Maintaining ribbed border, P across to underarm. Slip sts of back from holder to free needle. P across. Slip sts of left front to free needle. P across, maintaining border at edge.

Work back and forth in St St on these joined sts of the body, maintaining the front borders and making buttonholes in the left front until the piece measures 5¼ inches from the underarm. Change to size 1 needles and work 1 inch in K 1, P 1 ribbing. Bind off in ribbing.

FINISHING
Sew sleeve seams and attach buttons. Block.

Diamond-Patterned Cardigan

This dressy little cardigan has an eyelet diamond pattern trimming the front opening and extending around the entire lower edge and running around the sleeves just above the ribbing. The front opening has knitted-on facings with buttonholes worked in them. It has good baby proportions and fits well.

If you are making it for a little girl, you might like to add an embroidered rosebud (see page 144) in each of the diamonds for a really special effect.

The sweaters in the photograph are exactly alike; one was turned over so the detailing on the back would be visible.

118

Six months

MATERIALS
Baby yarn, 1-ounce skeins, 3
Knitting needles, 1 pair size 2, 1 pair size 3
Buttons, white pearl, ¼ inch diameter, 5

GAUGE
8 sts = 1 inch on size 3 needles

INSTRUCTIONS

BACK
With size 2 needles, cast on 92 sts. Work in
K 1, P 1 ribbing for 12 rows. Change to size 3
needles.
Diamond pattern: Row 1: K 5, yo, skp, *K 2
tog, yo, K 9, yo, skp*, repeat between *'s to
within 7 sts of end. End row K 2 tog, yo, K 5.
Row 2 and all even rows: P.
Row 3: K 3, K 2 tog, yo, K 4, *yo, skp, K 5, K
2 tog, yo, K 4*, repeat to within 5 sts of end;
end row yo, skp, K 3.
Row 5: K 2, K 2 tog, yo, K 6, *yo, skp, K 3, K
2 tog, yo, K 6*, repeat to within 4 sts of end;
finish row yo, skp, K 2.
Row 7: K 1, K 2 tog, yo, K 8, *yo, skp, K 1, K
2 tog, yo, K 8*, repeat to within 3 sts of end.
End row yo, skp, K 1.
Row 9: K 2 tog, yo, *K 10, yo, sl 1, K 2 tog,
psso, yo*, repeat to within 11 sts of end. Finish row K 10, yo, K 1.

Work remainder of the back in St St as
follows: Work even until the piece measures
5½ inches above the ribbing. End with a K
row. Mark for underarm.
Armholes: Bind off 3 sts at beg of next 2 rows.
P 1 row.

Dec row: Skp, K to within 2 sts of end, K 2
tog. Repeat dec row every second row 2
times (79 sts).
Work even until 4½ inches above underarm marker; end with a K row.
Shoulders: Bind off 8 sts at beg of next 6 rows.
Slip remaining 31 sts to holder for neck ribbing.

RIGHT FRONT:
With size 2 needles, cast on 58 sts.
Row 1: K 5, sl as if to K (turning st), K 5, *P
1, K 1*, repeat between *'s to end.
Row 2: Work in K 1, P 1 ribbing to within 11
sts of end. P 11.

Repeat these two rows until 6 rows have
been completed.
Buttonhole row: K 2, yo, K 2 tog, K 1, sl 1, K 1,
K 2 tog, yo, K 2; work ribbing to end. (Repeat buttonhole row every 22nd row to
neck.)

Work even until 12 rows of ribbing have
been completed. Change to size 3 needles.
Diamond pattern: Retain the border and facing pattern (K 5, sl as if to K, K 5) all the way
to the neck edge. The instructions for the
balance of the two front pieces begin and
end with only the word *border* to indicate
this.
Row 1: Border, *K 2 tog, yo, K 9, yo, skp*,
repeat across row ending K 2 tog, yo, K 6.
Row 2 and all even rows: P.
Row 3: Border, K 2, *yo, skp, K 5, K 2 tog,
yo, K 4*, repeat across row ending yo, skp,
K 4.
Row 5: Border, K 3, *yo, skp, K 3, K 2 tog,
yo, K 6*, repeat across ending yo, skp, K 3.
Row 7: Border, K 4, *yo, skp, K 1, K 2 tog,
yo, K 8*, repeat across ending yo, skp, K 2.

Row 9: Border, K 5, *yo, sl 1, K 2 tog, psso, yo, K 10*, repeat across ending yo, skp, K 1.

Row 11: Border, K 3, K 2 tog, yo, K 3, yo, skp, K to end.

Row 13: Border, K 2, K 2 tog, yo, K 5, yo, skp, K to end.

Row 15: Border, K 1, K 2 tog, yo, K 7, yo, skp, K to end.

Row 17: Border, K 2 tog, yo, K 9, yo, skp, K to end.

Row 19: Border, K 2, yo, skp, K 5, K 2 tog, yo, K to end.

Row 21: Border, K 3, yo, skp, K 3, K 2 tog, yo, K to end.

Row 23: Border, K 4, yo, skp, K 1, K 2 tog, yo, K to end.

Row 25: Border, K 5, yo, sl 1, K 2 tog, psso, yo, K to end.

Repeat rows 11 through 25 until the piece is the same length as the back to the underarm (row 19 of third full diamond repeat). End with a K row. Mark for underarm.

Armhole: Bind off 3 sts at beg of next row, P to end. Work 2 rows even. Dec 1 st at end of next row. Repeat dec row every second row two times. Work even until 4½ inches above underarm marker. End at the front edge.

Neck and Shoulder : Row 1: Work 25 sts and sl to holder for neck ribbing; work to end.

Row 2: P.

Row 3: Skp, K to end.

Repeat rows 2 and 3 once (25 sts).

Row 6: Bind off 8 sts for shoulder, P to end.

Row 7: Skp, K to end.

Row 8: Repeat row 6.

Row 9: Skp, K to end. Bind off remaining sts.

Left Front: With size 2 needles, cast on 58 sts.

Row 1: P 1, K 1 ribbing to within 11 sts of end, K 5, sl 1, K 5. Work in ribbing maintaining front border for 12 rows. Change to size 3 needles.

As in the right front, maintain the 11 sts of the border to the neck but do not work buttonholes. Instructions for the rows read as for the right front.

Row 1: K 5, yo, skp, *K 2 tog, yo, K 9, yo, skp*, repeat to within 12 sts of end, finish row K 1 plus border.

Row 2 and all even rows: P.

Row 3: K 3, K 2 tog, yo, K 4, *yo, skp, K 5, K 2 tog, yo, K 4*, repeat to within 14 sts of border, end K 3 plus border.

Row 5: K 2, K 2 tog, yo, K 6, *yo, skp, K 3, K 2 tog, yo, K 6*, repeat to within 15 sts of end, finish K 4 plus border.

Row 7: K 1, K 2 tog, yo, K 8, *yo, skp, K 1, K 2 tog, yo, K 8*, repeat to within 16 sts of end, finish K 5 plus border.

Row 9: K 2 tog, yo, *K 10, yo, sl 1, K 2 tog, psso, yo*, repeat to within 17 sts of end, finish K 6 plus border.

Row 11: K 36, K 2 tog, yo, K 3, yo, skp, K 4 plus border.

Row 13: K 35, K 2 tog, yo, K 5, yo, skp, K 3 plus border.

Row 15: K 34, K 2 tog, yo, K 7, yo, skp, K 2 plus border.

Row 17: K 33, K 2 tog, yo, K 9, yo, skp, K 1 plus border.

Row 19: K 35, yo, skp, K 5, K 2 tog, yo, K 3 plus border.

Row 21: K 36, yo, skp, K 3, K 2 tog, yo, K 4 plus border.

Row 23: K 37, yo, skp, K 1, K 2 tog, yo, K 5 plus border.

Row 25: K 38, yo, sl 1, K 2 tog, psso, yo, K 6 plus border.

Repeating rows 11 through 25, work to

correspond to the right front, reversing the shaping at the armhole.

Neck and Shoulder: Row 1: Work to within 25 sts of end, sl last 25 sts to the holder for neck ribbing.

Row 2: P.

Row 3: Work to within 2 sts of end, K 2 tog.

Complete to correspond to right front, reversing the shaping for the shoulder.

SLEEVES

With size 2 needles, cast on 43 sts. Work in K 1, P 1 ribbing for 12 rows. Change to size 3 needles.

Row 1: K 2, *K 2 tog, yo, K 9, yo, skp*, repeat between *'s ending K 2.

Row 2 and all even numbered rows: P.

Row 3: K 4, *yo, skp, K 5, K 2 tog, yo, K 4*, repeat to end.

Row 5: K 5, *yo, skp, K 3, K 2 tog, yo, K 6*, repeat ending K 5.

Row 7: K 6, *yo, skp, K 1, K 2 tog, yo, K 8*, repeat ending K 6.

Row 9: K 7, *yo, sl 1, K 2 tog, psso, yo, K 10*, repeat ending K 7.

Row 10: P.

Row 11: Inc row: Inc 1 st in first st, K to within 2 sts of end, inc 1 st in next st, K 1.

Working in St St, repeat inc row every sixth row seven times (57 sts).

Work even until 6 inches above ribbing, end with a K row. Bind off 3 sts at beg of next 2 rows.

Dec row: K 2 tog, K to within 2 sts of end, skp. Repeat dec row every second row six times. Bind off 2 sts at beg of each of next 8 rows. Bind off remaining sts.

NECK RIBBING

Beginning at the left front edge, sl from holders to size 2 needle 25 sts of left front and 31 sts of back. Beginning at the right front edge, sl 25 sts of right front to free size 2 needle, join yarn, and with this needle pick up and K 9 sts along right neck edge, K 31 sts of back, pick up 9 sts along left neck edge, work 25 sts of left front.

Maintaining the front borders and working a buttonhole in the first row of right front, work in K 1, P 1 ribbing for 6 rows. Bind off in ribbing.

FINISHING

Sew the shoulder seams. Pin sleeves in place and then sew. Beginning either at the cuff or the bottom edge, sew sleeves and underarm seam.

Turn the front facings to the inside along the slip st row and sew in place. Whip around buttonholes, working through both layers of facing. Attach buttons. Block.

TECHNIQUES

Heirloom Sewing

Heirloom Sewing—sometimes called French Hand Sewing—is a revitalization of the exquisite techniques used generations ago to create delicate clothing and linens. When sewing machines were introduced, the easier machine-stitched tucks became for many people more of a status symbol than tucks made by hand, but a few traditionalists still valued the delicacy and luxury of hand sewing, practiced it, and passed on the techniques. Today, with this elegant sewing just as with many other things in our lives, we have come full circle and once again use the old methods with new vigor and pleasure. Those of us who love and collect antique clothing recognize the aptness of the term Heirloom Sewing, for we cherish the handmade garments of yesteryear and feel sure that the handmades of today are the clothing that will be saved and used again in the future.

Since Heirloom Sewing is so appropriate for very special baby clothing, patterns for a fancy pillow (page 14), a dress and slip (page 18), and two button-on suits (pages 26 and 35) have been included in this book. Heirloom Sewing may also be used for day gowns, christening gowns, and bonnets for the baby. You will find this is an addictive kind of sewing and you will be proud of the things you create.

There are several important things to know about Heirloom Sewing before trying it. The first and most obvious is that it is done entirely by hand. This necessarily means that it is time-consuming and sometimes tedious. It is worth every bit of the effort entailed, but definitely not fast.

Another basic characteristic of Heirloom Sewing is that it must be practiced on fabrics woven of natural fibers—100 percent cotton, linen, silk, light-weight wool. The new blended fabrics are wonderful, but their springy textures make it impossible to roll and whip a hem, and without this basic construction method, lovely garments of the kind described in this book can hardly be created.

All the pieces of a garment in Heirloom Sewing must be cut exactly on the grain. Such careful work is time consuming, but essential to success. Each piece must be started on fabric that has been straightened by pulling threads and cutting on that line (see pages 124–25). Tucks must be marked by pulled threads. My method of construction is to make all tucks and to sew in all insertions or other trims on a rectangle of material before cutting it to the pattern shape needed.

MATERIALS

FABRICS

Fabrics made of natural fibers, essential for true Heirloom Sewing, are sometimes difficult to find, but they now are appearing more frequently in fine fabric stores. Some needlework shops also carry fabrics and laces. Look for batiste, lawn, pima broadcloth, and organdy of 100 percent cotton. Handkerchief linen, silk, and wool challis are also available. Batiste and lawn are best for baby clothing.

TRIMMINGS

Trimmings should also be all cotton, though an exception can be made of some laces which are currently being manufactured with 10 percent nylon. This small bit of synthetic does not seem to interfere with the sewing process.

Laces vary greatly in width and pattern. Lace edgings have one scalloped edge, one straight edge. Lace insertions have two straight edges. Embroidered edgings and insertions may also be used.

Entredeux is a ready-made trim which looks like a narrow row of hemstitching on a fine batiste strip (see illustration). It is used between fabric and trim or between two kinds of trimming—a literal translation of the name is "between two." It adds body and strength to many finishes and stabilizes gathers. In addition, it is a lovely trim in itself and should be used for this reason as much as for its utility.

Work in as much or as little entredeux as you like. It adds to the cost of materials for a project, but the use of this lovely little trim is a true hallmark of Heirloom Sewing. It is elegant in sleeve and yoke seams and between lace and insertions, and it is very necessary at the edges of puffing strips and ruffles.

Ribbon is used in lace insertions and beadings, for bonnet ties and sashes, and for bows. Double-faced satin is best for bonnet ties and sashes but single-faced is fine for insertion in a pillow or the skirt of a dress where only one side will ever show.

TOOLS

Needles must be very fine and sharp. In my experience, #10 crewel and #12 sharps work best. Keep a good supply, as sewing is easiest with a shiny new needle.

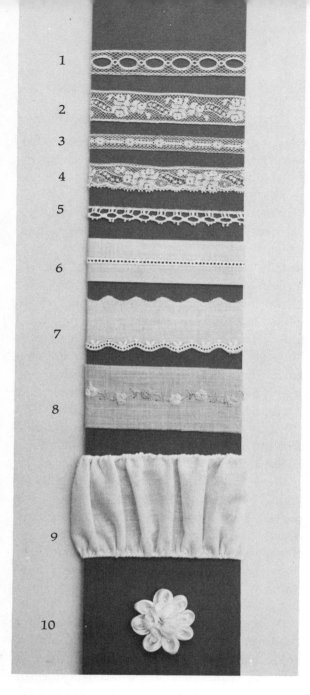

A small sampling of the lace and other trimming materials that can be used in Heirloom Sewing. 1. Lace beading. 2. and 3. Two widths of lace insertion. 4. Fine lace edging. 5. Heavy lace edging. 6. Entredeux. 7. Embroidered batiste edging. 8. Embroidered batiste insertion. 9. Puffing. 10. Ribbon Rosette.

Thread which is all cotton and very fine is best. A good size is 150, but sometimes 100 can be used. This thread is not generally stocked in fabric stores. Look for it in the needlework shop that carries natural fiber fabrics and laces. To strengthen the thread, pull it across beeswax after threading the needle.

Scissors need to be sharp—ordinary sewing and embroidery scissors are fine. The use of a thimble is optional. If you use one for other sewing, you will naturally want one for this fine handwork. If you feel a thimble is a bother, there is no need to burden yourself trying to use one.

PATTERNS

Patterns designed expressly for Heirloom Sewing are available in some of the stores which sell natural fiber fabrics. They are generally expensive but buying one is a good investment for many beginners as the patterns go into great detail about the construction of the garment they describe and usually include several collar styles or other variations. After using a commercial Heirloom Sewing pattern and the patterns in this book, you will understand how to adapt almost any kind of commercial pattern to Heirloom Sewing, and this is a great advantage.

CONSTRUCTION METHODS

CUTTING

Generally, all pieces should be cut from a square or rectangle of fabric which has been straightened by pulling a thread to mark the cutting line.

To straighten one end of a cut of fabric, clip the selvage at one side and pull a thread across the width. If the fabric is very fine or tightly woven, the thread may break. If so, try to find the end of the thread or take a parallel one and pull it. There is always some breakage, but with practice you will learn to minimize it. Use the line made by the pulled thread as a cutting guide.

Cut the small working pieces to the dimensions noted on the charts also by pulling threads for all sides.

In the drawings for pattern pieces in this book—the shirt front and sleeves for the Sunday Suit on page 26, for instance—the pattern piece itself is shown over a rectangle of fabric for which the dimensions are given. Lines on the rectangle or working piece show the layout for markings for tucks. The fabric should be cut to the size indicated, threads pulled to mark the tucks, tucks sewn, any insertion added, and any embroidery completed. The piece should then be pressed— washed if any traces of transfer pencil show after the embroidery. The pattern piece is then centered on the embellished fabric, the cutting line marked, and the tucks and insertion reinforced where the stitching crosses the cutting line; then finally the piece is cut. This method ensures perfect sizing and centering. It also establishes the procedure used for converting commercial patterns to Heirloom Sewing.

Sewing
Heirloom Sewing is hand sewing. Work in tiny running stitches and whipping stitches.

All seams should be French seams unless entredeux is being inserted—these should be rolled and whipped to the entredeux.

Seam allowances on the Heirloom patterns in the book are ¼ inch. This is somewhat narrower than the allowances in most commercial patterns, but adequate for this construction method.

Tucks
Following the pattern instructions, measure and mark for tucks along the top edge of the working piece. Pull a thread the length of each tuck. Fold the fabric on the line made by removing the thread, and stitch the tuck. (Some believe that removing the thread to mark the tuck weakens the fabric and should be avoided. With fine batistes and lawns I have not found this to be so, but an alternative is to pull the thread just enough to make a line in the fabric, then finger-press and stitch the tuck.)

Pin Tucks: Are usually marked ½ inch apart, folded on the line and stitched with small running stitches ⅛ inch from the fold.

Whipped Tucks: Are generally marked ½ inch apart but can be spaced more closely if desired. Pull a thread, fold on the line, and whip over the fold edge placing the stitches about 1/16 inch apart.

Wide Tucks: Serve different decorative purposes and can vary in width as needed. A series of ½-inch-wide tucks in the skirt of a little girl's dress makes lovely trim and can be released to lengthen the garment when needed.

Rolling and Whipping
Begin with fabric that has been cut on the

line of a pulled thread. Using a small needle threaded with cotton thread waxed and knotted at one end, and holding the needle in the right hand, begin to roll the edge for hemming. Hold the fabric with the wrong side facing you, the edge to be rolled at the top. Place the needle against the top right corner of the fabric, moisten the thumb and index finger of your other hand, and with these moistened fingers roll the fabric toward you down over the needle being held parallel to the edge of the fabric. Roll the fabric until the raw edge is completely covered—this should use up less than ¼ inch of fabric.

Slide the needle out of the roll. Hold the roll gently between the thumb and forefinger of your right hand while continuing to roll the balance of the edge with your left. Moisten your fingers as often as necessary to keep the roll in place. If the roll seems uneven, continue working—it will get better. Soon rolling will be an automatic process for you and your work will be straight and even.

Roll the entire edge before beginning to stitch. Insert the needle under the roll; holding the needle at a 45-degree angle, come out at the top of the roll. Make your stitches small—less than ⅛ inch apart. Do not catch the fabric behind the roll in the stitch. Simply insert the needle under the roll and bring it out at the top.

After making five or six stitches, check to see if your work is correct by pulling the fabric along the stitches, as if to gather. If the piece gathers, the stitches are correct. If it will not gather, fabric has been caught in with the roll and this means that the stitching must be corrected.

GATHERING

Gathering for ruffles, puffing, and embroidered edgings is worked as in the rolling and hemming process. Work a few inches, pull up to the desired fullness, work a few more inches, gather, and continue thus to the end of the piece.

PUFFING

This elegant old self-trim is rarely seen today except in Heirloom Sewing. It consists simply of a narrow piece of fabric gathered on both edges and used like an insertion. When using, it is best to use entredeux on both sides between the puffing and the base fabric to stabilize the gathers and make a firm seam.

To make a puffing strip, decide first the length and width of the finished piece. Cut a strip of fabric at least twice—but not more than two and one-half times—as long as and ½-inch wider than the finished measurements. Strips may be pieced together if necessary with narrow French seams.

Roll, whip, and gather both edges of the strip. Use a paper guide if necessary to help distribute the gathers evenly. Whip entredeux to both rolled and gathered edges.

Ruffles: Cut ruffles from twice to two and one-half times as long as and ½-inch wider than the finished piece should be. Roll and whip one side, attaching all lace, insertions, or trim that will adorn the hem edge of the ruffle. Roll and gather the other edge to the needed measurement.

ATTACHING LACE TO ROLLED EDGE

Lace or an insertion which is to be applied

without gathering can be sewn to a rolled edge at the same time the initial rolling and hemming are done. Simply roll the edge as for a plain hem. When you begin to whip the edge, do so with the lace over the index finger along the roll. Catch a thread of the lace edge with each whipping stitch.

If the lace is to be gathered, pull one of the heavy threads on the straight edge to gather the lace to the desired fullness. Hold the gathered lace next to the roll and catch the edge with the whipping stitches.

ATTACHING ENTREDEUX TO ROLLED EDGE

Entredeux comes with about ½ inch of raw-edged batiste on each side of the stitching. This edge is cut away as close as possible to the stitching before the entredeux is attached to the fabric or trim.

To attach entredeux to a rolled hem, cut away the batiste on one side, hold the entredeux next to the rolled edge, and catch one square of the entredeux with each whipping stitch.

If the entredeux is to be used in a seam, the raw edge of each of the pieces to be joined must be rolled and whipped to the trimmed entredeux. This is fairly easy in a perfectly straight seam. If the two pieces to be joined are shaped—for example, a sleeve and an armhole—the rolling is a bit more difficult but can be accomplished with a little practice. The resulting seam is strong and very decorative.

To apply entredeux to the gathered edge of either a puffing strip or a ruffle, simply whip it to the edge, making one stitch in each square of the entredeux.

ADDITIONAL DETAILS

Press each piece as it is completed and press all seams as they are sewn, just as in other fine sewing. Utilize other basic sewing techniques for small details—make handmade buttonholes and belt loops, use very fine quality buttons, ribbon, and other trim, and so forth.

RIBBON ROSETTES

Ribbon rosettes are a pretty and traditional trim for Heirloom Sewing. They are elegant on bonnets, pillows, dresses, and lingerie. Part of their charm is that they look so delightfully complicated but are in fact very easy to make.

The prettiest ones are made from 1-inch-wide double-faced satin ribbon. For a size that looks right on baby clothing, cut a 10-inch length of ribbon. Begin to mark the ribbon to correspond to the piece shown on the diagram by measuring in from the left end ½ inch and placing a very light pencil mark on one edge of the ribbon. From that mark, measure and mark the balance of the strip at 1-inch intervals. On the other edge of the ribbon, make similar marks placed exactly halfway between the first dots.

RIBBON ROSETTE

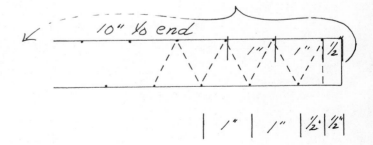

QUILTED SACQUE (PAGE 42), DETAIL SHOW-
ING THE QUILTING, FEATHER STITCH EMBROI-
DERY, LACE EDGING, AND RIBBON ROSETTES.

With a fine needle and waxed thread, make a line of small running stitches connecting the dots as shown on the diagram. Do not fasten off the thread at the end; leave it for the moment. Thread another needle and sew the two ends of the ribbon together in a seam utilizing the ½-inch of material left at either end. Fasten off this thread.

Using the first thread, pull up gathers to form the rosette. Turn the rosette over to the back and fasten the points together with a whipping stitch.

When using rosettes to trim bonnet ties where they are attached to the cap, first sew the ties in place, then sew the rosette over the end.

Knitting

Prince Charles, in a press interview several months after the announcement that he and Princess Diana would be parents, noted happily that the couple had received as gifts from the British people dozens of books of advice about "parenting" as well as "thousands of booties and cardigans too numerous to count." His obvious pleasure in the love and industry that produced the hand-knit bounty emphasized the way news of a baby starts needles clicking everywhere. Grandmothers, aunts, and friends all want immediately to knit something little, precious, and special. Mothers-to-be love receiving these gifts, dreaming over them and displaying them to other well-wishers.

Baby hand-knits are fun to make and delightful to receive, but they are also infinitely practical. Yarns chosen carefully can be softer and more luxurious than those found in ready-mades, and there is no question that a hand-knit garment is of better basic construction than one knit commercially. The few handmades found in boutiques and stores sell for astronomically high prices.

Knitters everywhere, however, know that one does not knit a sacque or booties for a new baby to save money or simply because they are nicer than items purchased in a store. We do it because it allows us to give something that no one else can give—part of ourselves—and in that giving there is great joy.

When choosing yarn for your baby gift, look for the best quality to be found. A tiny sweater takes only about three ounces, so you can afford to buy the best. Generally the best-known brands—but not the discount store brands—are better buys. They are usually a softer spin, come in matched dye lots, and have slightly better yardages. Buy the practical synthetics and don't even dream about the wonderful wools we used to have. They were lovely but had to be carefully washed to prevent shrinkage and had to be blocked flat. A gift made of wool yarn may be prized, but more than likely it will be condemned to staying in the drawer unless there is a willing grandmother to do the washing.

Although angora, mohair, and other fuzzy yarns are pretty and tempting, avoid them. Even a baby who is not allergic to the fibers will sneeze and be annoyed by the fuzzies that come off the sweater. A little bit for embroidery or trim is pretty and probably won't be a problem, but if you are making the sweater or booties of easy-care yarn, make the trim of easy-care material also.

The name Baby Yarn on a label indicates both its primary use and its weight. Most Baby Yarns are three-ply—three very fine strands twisted into one heavier strand—but some are two-ply and still the same weight. Baby Yarn usually knits to a gauge of seven and one half to eight stitches per inch on a size 3 needle or nine stitches to the inch on a size 2 needle. These average knitting gauges usually appear on the label for comparison to those required by the knitting pattern.

Sport Yarn is the common designation for the other weight yarn used for the patterns in this book. It is usually also a two- or three-ply yarn, but knits up to a heavier product. Check the gauge on the label when buying to make certain you will be able to get the number of stitches per inch your pat-

tern requires. Most Sport Yarns work up to an average seven stitches to the inch on a size 4 needle.

Always buy enough of one dye lot to complete your garment. Many shops suggest buying an extra skein and will accept unopened skeins for refund or exchange within a reasonable time. Buying the extra skein is a good idea although knit-aholics find it never goes back since it is so handy for extra booties, mittens, and other goodies.

The label on yarn is the best source for reliable instructions for its care. Both washing and drying instructions should be carefully followed for best results. Some thoughtful knitters enclose a yarn label and a few yards of yarn in the package with a gift knit. The yarn may be needed later for mending or sewing on a button, and the instructions on the label leave no doubt about how to handle the knit when the time comes to clean it. Both are very much appreciated.

The importance of knitting to the correct stitch gauge cannot be overemphasized. This is the only way to ensure the perfect fit envisioned in the design and instructions. Before beginning any project, check your gauge with the needles and yarn specified.

Knit a 3-inch square. Measure carefully and count the number of stitches to the inch—the number of rows, too, if specified.

If your number of stitches is less than required, change to smaller needles and try again. If the number of stitches you count is greater than that called for, your work is too tight and you need to try larger needles.

Most knitting instructions call for slightly more yarn than is actually needed simply because it is impossible to design a garment that finishes up at exactly the end of a skein. There may be any portion of that last skein left over, but you should not come up short if you have followed the instructions carefully and knit to the gauge specified.

You will note that all my bootie patterns call for one skein of Baby Yarn, because you can't buy less. Experienced knitters know that it may be possible to get two pair from a skein or that yarn left over from a sacque may be enough for a pair of booties. The ability to make these judgments improves with experience, but this knitter admits to sometimes miscalculating—thinking that enough yarn remains to make something else, and then later having to search the yarn shops trying to match a dye lot to finish just a few rows. Taking such risks is one aspect of needle-mania; people bitten by the mania eventually learn to cope with its consequences.

Many of the new synthetic yarns need no blocking or shaping, but a touch-up with the steam iron always adds a professionally finished look. An added and appreciated gesture for a baby gift is to hand-wash the garment in gentle detergent so it is ready for the baby to wear. I use the favorite old baby soap flakes in warm water, rinse very well, avoid wringing, roll in a towel, squeeze to remove most of the water, then dry flat on a towel, shaping the garment while wet. A final gentle touch-up with the steam iron makes it look like the picture in the book.

KNITTING ABBREVIATIONS

K	knit
P	purl
tog	together
skp	slip, knit, pass
st(s)	stitch(es)
dec	decrease
inc	increase
beg	beginning
yo	yarn over
psso	pass slipped st(s) over
sl	slip
St St	stockinette stitch
Gtr St	garter stitch

BISHOP CORD TIES

To make Bishop Cord Ties for booties or other projects, cut a 2-yard length of yarn. Fold in half and tie cut ends in a knot. Hook the looped end over a chair finial or ask someone to hold it for you. Insert a finger in the loop at the knotted end and twist the yarn tightly up to the finial.

Take hold of the twisted strand at the middle, slide the end off the finial, and fold the cord in half, allowing it to twist. Knot the loose ends.

This cord is very practical for booties and bonnet ties as it washes with the garment and needs no pressing or touch-up.

Embroidery for Baby

Embroidery on baby garments, nursery accessories, and gifts can be as varied as the projects themselves. The working methods and techniques are those of traditional embroidery. No exact formula prescribes which stitches or colors must be used or even indicates the size or scale of the stitches, these generally being dictated by the overall design and the preference of the embroiderer. Naturally, the crewel border on a wool christening blanket should be worked with a heavier thread and larger stitches than those used on a dainty batiste gown or shirt, but there is still much leeway.

Fabrics and materials, especially those used in Heirloom Sewing, are expensive; hand construction is tedious and time-consuming. It follows that embroidery details should be worked with care. Beautifully worked embroidery is often the final ingredient that binds painstaking construction and lovely fabric into an elegant whole. If the embroidery is perfect, one instinctively trusts what lies beneath it.

Embroidery, too, is often one last expression of the love that has gone into making the entire baby gift. Even if the gift is small, embroidery makes it a gift that only the maker could give. Such gifts are the ones that are treasured and used with the most joy and appreciation. Your embroidery is important; enjoy working it and give it with the pride and love it deserves.

Do the special embroidery for baby utilizing the skills and techniques you have perfected and enjoy. Work as you ordinarily do, using a hoop and thimble if that is your preference. Begin and end threads wherever possible without knots so the wrong side of the work is neat.

You will find that the patterns and charts in this book allow you to duplicate exactly the finished media models photographed. Full-size patterns for the embroidery designs permit you to trace them and work without the tiresome—and often unsuccessful—process of enlarging. Charts indicate the placement of colors and stitches, and the instructions are detailed enough to make the construction and embroidery processes easy.

Fabric requirements are stated as precisely as possible. When only a small piece of fabric is needed, as for the Birth Record (see page 85), its exact dimensions are given to allow the use of materials you may have on hand. Thread quantities are based on those used to complete the projects as shown. Some thread may be left over, but small surpluses as a margin of safety are part of the natural process of embroidery.

Transfer pencils make it easy to trace a design and fix it on the fabric ready to embroider. Look for them in needlework shops and craft stores. Some can be removed with soap and water, others require dry-cleaning fluid. For baby projects, I prefer washable pencils so if any pencil traces remain when the embroidery is finished, they can be washed out before the garment is constructed.

To transfer a design from the book to fabric, use the transfer pencil to trace the full-size drawing on a good grade of tracing paper or parchment. The paper should be heavy enough to withstand the heat of your iron when transferring. Keep the pencil sharp so the lines are thin and easily covered with embroidery. If you make a drawing mistake, discard the paper and begin over to avoid transferring the error to the fabric.

If the design is divided over two pages, match the sections by lining up the slashed lines and other guides noted in the instructions for the project.

It is usually a good idea to make a small test transfer first. Using a sample sketch and a scrap of fabric you'll be using, make sure the pencil marking transfers properly and that the heat of the iron does not scorch the fabric through the tracing paper. If some scorching does occur on the test piece, protect your final fabric by putting a second piece of tracing paper over the transfer pattern.

The directions for each project indicate the exact embroidery materials used in the model shown in the photograph. Most threads are cotton embroidery floss to keep the garments washable; any good, reliable brand may be used. When identical coloring is needed for best effect, DMC color numbers for that brand of thread have been noted. Since most brands carry only color numbers for identification, I have added general color names (medium blue, pale blue, etc.) to help with substitution. Thread requirements are based on the familiar 8-yard skein.

EMBROIDERY STITCHES

The stitches of embroidery are many and varied. To make the baby garments in this book, only a few have been utilized, all of them familiar and easily worked. They are diagrammed here only for your reference, not as a complete stitch vocabulary.

A photograph for each stitch shows a few completed stitches, the needle inserted as if to continue, the thread in the proper position. The result is clear and graphic, almost as helpful as having a teacher sitting beside you demonstrating the stitches. For the purpose of clear photographic reproduction, heavy thread was used in making the sample stitches, which therefore appear much larger than your final stitches will be when you are working with the embroidery floss in most of the baby projects.

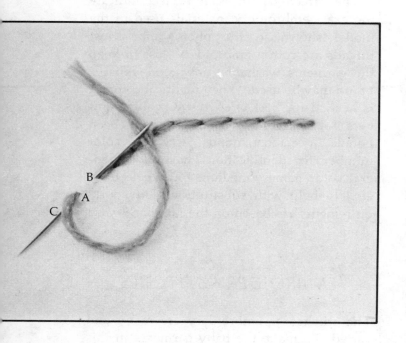

BACK STITCH

An easy outline stitch, the Back Stitch makes a neat line that looks very much like the top of a row of machine stitching. It may be used as a finishing edge or outline or can be worked in closely spaced rows to create a solid filling. Worked very small, it is an ideal stitch for lettering and curved outlines. As a foundation under stitches like Satin, it adds padding and makes it possible to work very smooth edges.

To begin a row of stitches, bring the needle to the surface at *a* (as indicated in the photograph), which is one stitch length from the beginning of the row, and pull the thread through. Go down at *b* and return to the surface at *c*, keeping the distance from *a* to *b* and *a* to *c* equal. Pull the yarn through to form a stitch. Insert the needle again at *a* and continue stitching, keeping the stitches uniform in length.

BACK STITCH, WHIPPED

This embellishment of the Back Stitch adds another color without making the line much wider. It can be used in most situations where the plain Back Stitch would be appropriate.

Work a row of Back Stitch. Using a new color, bring the needle to the surface near the center of the first stitch and pull the yarn through. Without piercing the fabric, whip along the row as shown.

BULLION KNOT

Although a bit tricky at first, once mastered the Bullion Knot is a stitch you will use often and for many different purposes. It can be made to lie flat along a line, or to curve, or to form a rosebud cluster, a very appropriate trim on baby garments.

To begin, bring the needle up at *a* and pull the yarn through. Go down at *b* and come up again at *a* but do not pull the thread through. Wrap the yarn around the needle until the length of the coil is roughly the distance from *a* to *b*.

Hold the wrap firmly and pull the needle through the coil of yarn. Hold the wrap and pull the yarn all the way through so the stitch lies flat on the fabric. Take the needle to the wrong side at *b*.

If the yarn is wrapped around the needle so the coil is the same length as the distance from *a* to *b*, the stitch will lie flat on the fabric. To make a curved stitch, wrap the yarn around the needle a few more times and finish the stitch in the usual manner.

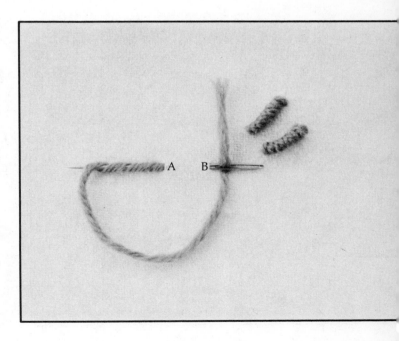

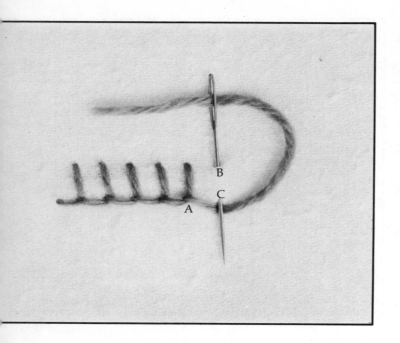

BUTTONHOLE OR BLANKET STITCH

The Buttonhole Stitch, also called the Blanket Stitch, can be worked with the loops widely and evenly spaced as shown in the photograph, or in many variations that group the stitches in decorative patterns.

To work, bring the needle up at *a* and pull the yarn through. Holding the yarn beneath the needle to form a loop, insert the needle into the fabric at *b* and bring it back to the surface at *c*. Pull the needle through, adjusting the tension of the loop to allow the stitch to lie flat. Continue in this manner.

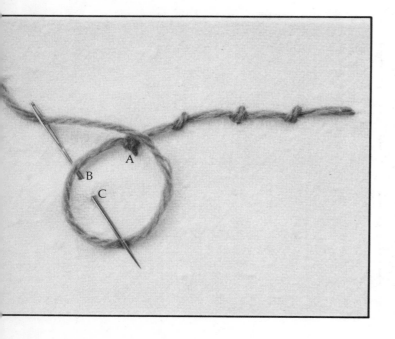

CORAL STITCH

The Coral Stitch makes a pretty outline, with its little knots to accent the line. A favorite with early American embroiderers, this is a lovely way to outline a leaf or accent an edge.

To work, bring the yarn up at *a* and pull through. Lay the yarn along the stitching line to the left and make a loop as shown. Hold in place with your thumb. Insert the needle at *b* and bring to the surface at *c*, making a small, slanting stitch. With the lower part of the loop under the needle, pull the yarn through to form a knot. Continue from the beginning.

CROSS STITCH

Equally at home on canvas or fabric, the Cross Stitch is easy but also beautiful and effective. The secret of perfect Cross Stitch is always to have the base stitches slanting in one direction throughout the work.

To work a row of stitches, bring the needle to the surface at *a* and pull the yarn through. Insert the needle at *b* and bring it up again at *c*, which is directly below *b* and to the right on the same line as *a*. Pull the yarn through to form the slanted stitch. Continue to the end of the row. Return by working as shown, inserting the needle and bringing it to the surface in the same holes made by the previous stitches.

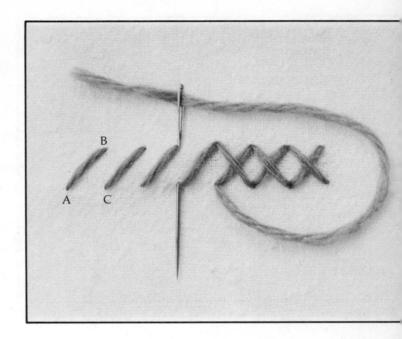

FEATHER STITCH

Making a wardrobe of lovely baby clothing without the Feather Stitch would be hard indeed. The stitch has long been a favorite for trimming all manner of little things and is most treasured by stitchers.

To begin, work from right to left or top to bottom. Bring the needle to the surface at *a* and pull the yarn through. Lay the yarn flat and hold in place with your thumb. Insert the needle at *b* and bring it up at *c* with the loop of yarn in the position shown in the photograph. Pull the yarn through. Holding the yarn flat again and making the loop in the opposite direction, insert the needle on the opposite side at *d*, bring it out again at *e* and pull through to form a loop. Repeat to desired length.

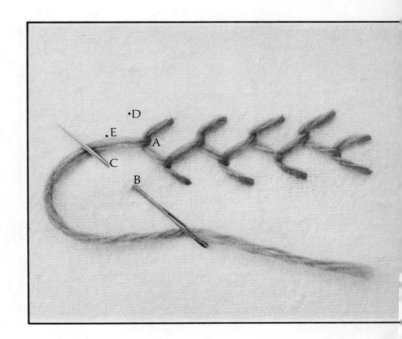

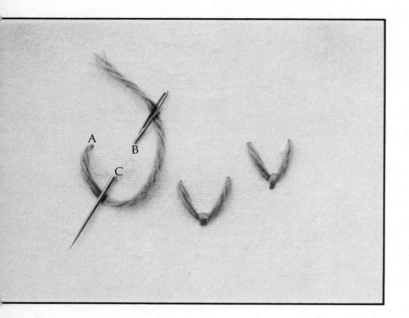

FLY STITCH

The Fly Stitch is most often used as a light filling. The tie-down stitch that secures it can be made any length that is needed.

To begin, bring the needle up at *a*, pulling the thread through. With the yarn in the position shown, go down at *b* and come up at *c*. Pull the yarn through and adjust the loop so it lies flat but is not stretched. Make a small tie-down stitch over the loop at *c*.

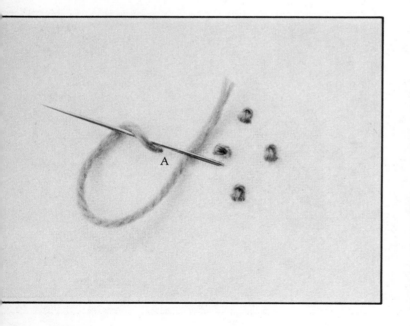

FRENCH KNOT

This interesting little knot serves many purposes, and gives to embroidery much of its charm.

To make the knot, bring the needle to the surface at *a* and pull the yarn through. Wrap the yarn around the needle once; then insert the tip of the needle into the fabric close to *a* but with at least one thread intervening. Pull the yarn to tighten the loop snugly around the needle. Pull the needle through to the back of the work.

HERRINGBONE STITCH

The Herringbone Stitch is good for wide lines and borders, and also as a filling. Worked on the wrong side, it is the stitch used for shadow work like that on the comforter on page 60.

To work, begin at the left by bringing the yarn to the surface at *a* and pulling it through. With the yarn in the position shown, insert the needle at *b* and bring it out at *c*. Pull it through. Throw the yarn to the top, insert the needle at *d*, and bring it to the surface at *e*. Repeat to complete the row.

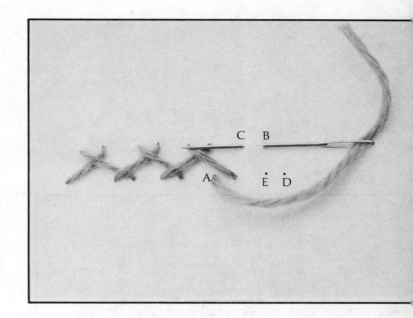

LAZY DAISY STITCH

Sometimes called the Detached Chain, this is an easy, versatile stitch that can add many details to embroidery for a baby. It can be used for lovely little flowers and leaves or it can be utilized in Crazy Quilt patterns in numerous ways.

To work, bring the needle up at *a* and pull the yarn through. Holding the yarn below the needle to form a loop, go down again at *a* and bring the needle to the surface at *b*. Pull the yarn through and adjust the loop. Make a small stitch across the loop at *b* to fasten it.

LONG AND SHORT STITCH

Although most often associated with wool yarns and crewel embroidery, the Long and Short is a useful stitch for other threads and makes a perfect filling for areas which need a little texture—for example, the animals in the Birth Record on page 85. When used thus with just one color thread, the stitch direction can be adjusted to give the illusion of depth and roundness. Working the stitches in a random manner rather than in the even pattern generally used for crewel shading also helps suggest depth.

Long and Short is often confusing to the beginning stitcher because only the first or outside row contains both long and short stitches. In the balance of the work the stitches should be basically the same length.

Begin with a straight edge and make the long stitches ½ inch and the short ones half that length, spacing the stitches as shown in the photograph. In the next row, work all the stitches ½ inch long, placing them between the stitches of the first row and working through the end of the short stitches as indicated. Practice this for a few rows.

To work in a random pattern as for the animals in the Ribbons-and-Toys Birth Record, use the basic stitching pattern but shape the objects by stitching in a direction to create a rounded appearance and vary the stitch lengths slightly so there is an overall texture rather than an evenness of rows. A row of Split Stitch around the area to be worked is an invaluable aid in creating a smooth edge.

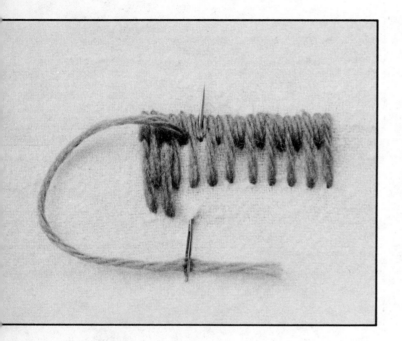

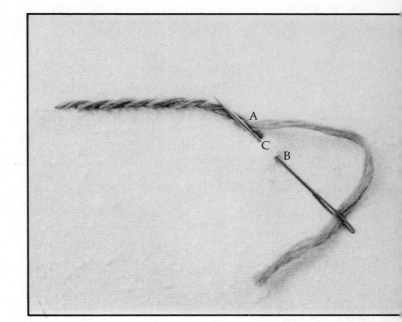

OUTLINE STITCH

Worked as shown in the photograph with the thread always above the needle, the Outline Stitch creates a fine line of close stitches.

To begin a line of stitches, bring the needle to the surface at *a* and pull the yarn through. With the yarn above the needle, go down at *b* and come up at *c* exactly halfway between *a* and *b*. Pull the yarn through and continue stitching.

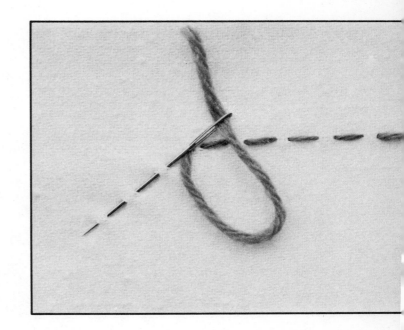

RUNNING STITCH

The Running Stitch is a basic sewing stitch, good also for embroidery when a fine, light line is needed. It may also be worked back and forth in rows to make a light filling.

Work as shown in the photograph, keeping the length of the stitches on the right side of the embroidery longer than those on the back. Try to maintain an even stitch length.

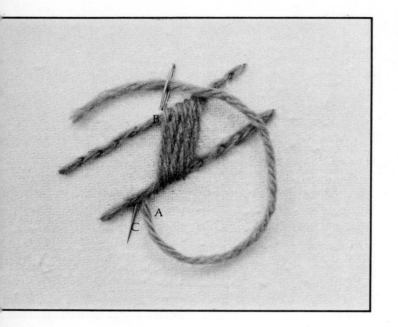

SATIN STITCH

One of the loveliest of embroidery stitches, Satin is aptly named, for when it is properly worked, it has a smooth, lustrous look. A Split Stitch outline underneath adds depth and eases the task of making an even outside edge. On baby clothing, Satin Stitch detail adds a look of elegance.

To work as photographed, outline the area with Split Stitch in the color that will be used for the Satin Stitch. Begin the Satin Stitch by bringing the needle to the surface at *a* and pulling the yarn through. Make a slanting stitch by taking the needle down at *b* and bringing it up again at *c*, which is close to *a*. Pull the yarn through and continue stitching until the area is covered.

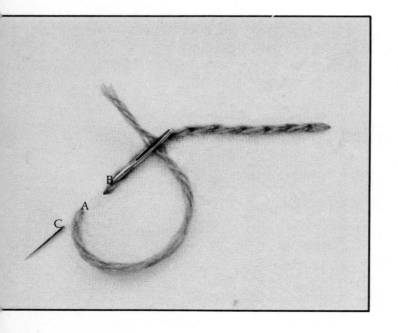

SPLIT STITCH

Hardworking little Split Stitch, which looks very much like a scaled down version of the Chain Stitch, does many embroidery jobs. It is a lovely, fine outlining stitch, is often used as padding under other stitches, and can be worked in closely spaced rows to make a solid filling.

To start, bring the needle up at *a* and pull the yarn through. Go down at *b* and come up at *c*, keeping the space between *a* and *c* equal to that between *a* and *b*. Insert the needle down into the center of this stitch, splitting it as shown in the photograph. Continue across the area.

STRAIGHT STITCH

The Straight Stitch is an uncomplicated flat stitch often used as an accent or scattered as seeding to add texture to a large, otherwise plain area. The slant and size of the stitches can vary to suit the need.

To work, simply place the stitches at the desired angle, following the stitching order from *a* to *b* to *c*.

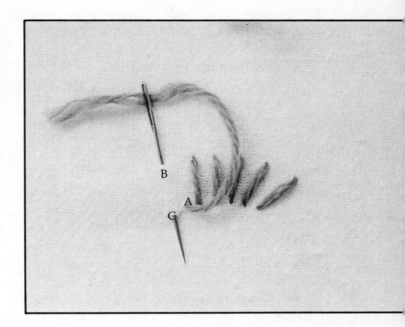

TRELLIS COUCHING

Trellis Couching quickly covers a large area with interesting pattern. The laid and couching threads can be of matching color or of contrasting color. The latter may take the simple upright form shown in the photograph, or may be Cross Stitch, Lazy Daisy or any one of a number of small stitches that would hold the laid threads in place. The diamond-shaped openings can be left plain as in the photograph or may be decorated with a small detached stitch.

To begin lay the long Straight Stitches in diagonal parallel lines, filling the shape of the motif. Bring the needle threaded with the couching thread to the surface at *a* and pull the yarn through. Make the tie-down stitch by inserting the needle at *b* and bringing it up again at *c* in position for the beginning of the next stitch. Tie each intersection of the laid threads with these stitches.

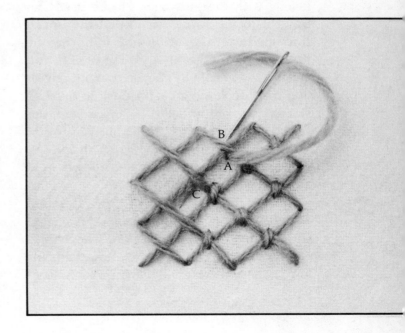

EMBROIDERED ROSEBUDS

Delicate rosebuds are a favorite kind of baby embroidery, adding a touch of color to all types of garments. Although there are several other methods of making these little trimmings, the following are my favorites.

STYLE 1

Begin with an oval of Satin Stitch. Make it slightly raised by working over padding or by working the stitches very close together and then making several stitches on top of the center.

This oval can be of the darkest shade of color to be used or it can be yellow. If working in only one color, use the darkest shade for the center and work outward to the lightest value. Usually three shades of a color are sufficient for a rosebud.

After completing the center, thread the needle with the next shade to be used and bring it to the surface at *a*. Pull the thread through. Insert the needle at *b* and bring the tip to the surface at *a*. Wrap the thread around the needle as shown, making one or two trips depending on the desired finished size of the rosebud. Tie off the thread and repeat the wrap with the lightest shade of thread. Taking care not to disturb the wraps, make two small stitches at the sides to hold all the wraps in place.

This style was used on the Rosebud Sacque and Booties (page 113) and on the Christening Blanket (page 45). The photograph of the embroidery detail on the blanket shows the rosebud worked with wool yarn.

STYLE 2

This is a dainty compact rosebud made simply from four Bullion Knots. Begin with two Bullion Knots of the center color placed close together and lying parallel to each other as in Step 1. These can be yellow or the darker of two shades of one color.

Assuming the center Bullion Knots were of the darker shade of two to be used, work two longer stitches in the lighter shade, placing them on either side of the first two. Wrap the needle generously for these two so they will curve slightly.

The Smocked Bonnet (page 24) is trimmed with several rosebuds worked in this fashion.

STYLE 3

This larger rosebud is an enlargement of the one in Style 2. To make, complete the Style 2 rosebud. Continue to add Bullion Knots around the original four, placing them so they curve around them and overlap. Shade color from the deepest shade at the center to the palest at the outside.

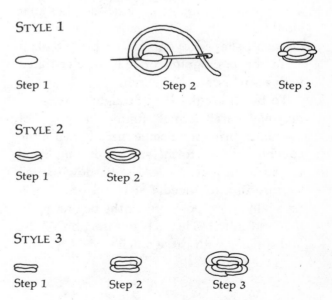

STYLE 1

Step 1   Step 2   Step 3

STYLE 2

Step 1   Step 2

STYLE 3

Step 1   Step 2   Step 3